6 $\underline{95}$

D1489624

The Minister's Funeral Handbook

The Minister's Funeral Handbook

A Complete Guide to Professional and Compassionate Leadership

Robert Blair

 **BAKER BOOK HOUSE**
Grand Rapids, Michigan 49516

Copyright 1990 by
Baker Book House Company

ISBN: 0-8010-0984-7

Printed in the United States of America

Unless otherwise indicated, Scripture quotations are taken from the New
International Version, copyright 1973, 1978 by the International Bible Society.
Used with permission of Zondervan Bible Publishers. Other versions used are RSV
(Revised Standard Version) and LB (The Living Bible).

The Macmillan Publishing Company has given permission to use the following
poetry of W. B. Yeats: "An Irish Airman Foresees His Death" and "When You Are
Old" from *The Poems of W. B. Yeats: A New Edition,* edited by Richard J. Finneran.
"Richard Cory" is taken from *The Children of the Night* by Edwin Arlington
Robinson, copyright 1897 by Charles Scribner's Sons, New York.

Virginia Vanderford has given permission to use the poetry of Pearl Pierson; the
Esta Bles eulogy is used with permission of Jeanne Bles; the William Dyerly material
is used with permission of Beverly Ann Dyerly; and Charlie Bradshaw has given permission to use the poem, "From the Heart."

Dedication

To my mother

Jessie Blair

who, with my late father
taught me the way of God

and to my wife

Norma

who has lovingly and faithfully
encouraged me in that way
for thirty-five years

Contents

Acknowledgments

It takes a lot of help from others to get a book to press.

I am indebted to so many:

Our church secretary, Margie Twyford, cheerfully, faithfully, and efficiently managed so many details and typed the poetry section.

Jeff and Pam Varga used their photographic skills to help make me look presentable.

Chuck Stokes gave me legal counsel.

Victoria Shellin's expert word processing and gentle wisdom was invaluable.

Pat Whisnant, my associate, read the manuscript and offered many helpful suggestions.

My cousin Virginia Vanderford provided additional poetry written by her mother, Pearl Pierson.

Our children Stephen, Rob, Stephanie, and Janice encouraged me constantly.

Introduction

Why should you read a book on how to prepare a funeral sermon? No one gets off this planet alive. Death is inevitable. And, if you are a minister, preparing funeral eulogies is an inevitable part of your ministry.

You will be called on repeatedly to help people confront death and adjust to their grief, to speak words of comfort, and to enable them to go on living positive lives. What you say and how you say it can make a dramatic difference in the recovery of the survivors. The confidence you demonstrate and the message you bring will not only help the mourners, it can also lead to your own spiritual well-being and renewal. I say this because death not only takes families by surprise, it also takes the clergy by surprise. Suppose you are surprised by a blowout on a strange road at night. If you have a jack, a spare tire, a flashlight, and a little mechanical knowledge you probably suffer only a mild inconvenience. If you lack these basic tools, you are in for some heavy-duty frustration. This book does not have every answer to every question, but what I have tried to do is inform you of situations you will face and to provide you with the basic tools that I have developed over the past thirty years.

This book is not only for ministers. The information should help anyone who is called to assist another in a time of grief. Often friends are guilty of giving the wrong advice about grief. They are usually present long before the minister or clergyperson. But what friends or ministers say and how they say it in those first few minutes can be crucial in the grieving process.

What qualifies me to write a book about funeral services and their preparation? It is more than just the experience of having done several hundred services over the past thirty years. Not everyone who is thrown into the water becomes an adept swimmer. In my case I was thrown in so many times and the experience was so painful that for sheer sake of survival it was necessary that I develop some skills.

Is it expertise? Only partially. Each funeral is different, having unique parameters of emotion, family interaction, expressions of guilt and grief. I'm always learning.

A few years ago I scheduled a memorial service for an old friend at our church building on Sunday afternoon. I asked a younger associate (not my present one) if he planned to attend so that he could gain some experience. He said that he had planned not to be present. His response indicated that he did not want to be at the building while a dead body was there. One day he will get his first request, as we all have, and he will "enjoy" that moment of sheer terror that many of us have experienced. Neither did I have any ambitions to be involved with funerals when I was young.

My first year of college was nearly an academic disaster. The following summer there were two significant changes in my life. First, following a stormy courtship, Norma finally agreed to marry me. Second, I decided to "become a minister."

The preacher who married us recommended that I attend a small Bible-based college in Oklahoma. It wasn't until my second semester there that I gained confidence in my academic abilities. However, at the time another event was shaping our lives: the birth of a son during my final exams in May.

Our funds were depleted. We rode the train home to Oregon. I had all the brashness and wisdom gleaned by any first-year Greek student. The little church where I grew up in Oregon did not have a preacher for a time, so I was employed by them to preach each Sunday.

That was my preparation, my training for the first funeral service I preached. I had attended only one funeral in my life, that of a distant cousin who had committed suicide in Europe about the close of World War II. I recall some of the emotion of that service in the church building in a little Kansas town, but at age nine I was far more curious about other things. I was not much affected by such a remote thing as death. Because of the length of time between the death and the funeral we all were "spared" seeing the open coffin.

I do have vivid recollections of tracts published by my well-intentioned brethren in Churches of Christ illustrating the teaching that proper baptism is burial in water. The only scriptural burial, they claimed, was dirt piled over one.

Did I hear sermons preached about funerals? I undoubtedly did. Did I see movies about funerals? Possibly, but I have no strong recollection or impression of them. I also suffered childhood nightmares of snakes and hellfire signifying death, but obviously I was ill prepared for helping others to confront death.

To many of our blue-collar friends in that Portland suburb, I was ostensibly a death expert. After all, I had been to Bible college. The irony is, even in working toward my B.A. and M.A. in Religion, I still had no training in conducting funerals, and I don't know if it is part of the curriculum of any college in our brotherhood. But my friends in the community did not know that, and within a short period of time they were calling on me to fulfill my "pastoral duty."

The first call was most tragic. A former high school friend, one year younger than I, had been killed in an auto accident. I was the only minister the family knew. His elder brother had perfect confidence in me. Today, thirty years later, I don't recall anything I said or might have said, or even where I got my resources. I believe I did call a couple of older minister friends to get their ideas on what to do and say. At some time I had picked up a minister's manual. However, my memory is not hazy on certain points. Vivid as though doubly etched yesterday is the recollection of my fear. It was a troubling, nauseating, morbid fear of death. I had not yet seen a corpse, and I was to be regarded as a "death expert."

I got to the funeral home early and was pacing back and forth through the lobby. The mortician was busy rearranging the chapel for the funeral in which I was to preach and wanted me out of the way. He escorted me to a little room off the lobby, suggesting that I meditate for a while. Without observing where I was, I sat down and began looking at my notes. I didn't look long. Right there in front of me, barely two feet away, was a corpse in a casket. It happened to be the remains of a woman in her midsixties, though I didn't stay long to gather details. I was out in the lobby again pacing the floor.

Did I offer any consolation to the family? I don't know. Did they receive any reassurance from the Word? I don't know that, either. But within a few days I got my second experience. An old family friend, a man in his late fifties, died of a heart attack one morning at work. I have no recollection of the service. I know one thing for sure. My fear of death was still unreasonably high.

At the end of another year my wife and I had saved sufficient funds so that we could move to Los Angeles where I finished school at Pepperdine College. As we were preparing to leave the Portland area, another old family friend, a woman in her early forties, was fighting a losing battle with cancer. Her condition was terminal. I prayed long, fervent prayers the week before we left not that God would heal her, but that the Lord would not let her die until we had moved. I did not want to have to deal with the reality of her death. The Lord did not grant my prayer.

After that, I was insulated from the problem for a while because of school and a brief tenure with an oil company. In 1963 I entered full-time ministry, but because I worked with an older, experienced minister funerals were usually his responsibility. In 1966 he died. Almost overnight I had to prepare a memorial service for him.

In the period since, I've eulogized hundreds of persons. I was on call for several years to two of the largest mortuaries in Southern California to do services for them in special circumstances.

Because Los Angeles is such a diverse community, I have been invited to do services for people of numerous ethnic and cultural backgrounds. I've eulogized some of my Jewish friends. There have been services for stillborn babies and infants, and services for older millionaires.

In the funerals I have conducted in recent years are certain things that I set out to accomplish. There are definite reasons for the funeral service beyond the need of the mortician to make a living. These have to do with using the sermon to proclaim the word about life in Jesus, to console the family by helping them remember the deceased, and to come to terms with death. All must be done in a proper order to be effective. In this small book I've offered suggestions on the minister's preparation of himself or herself as well as the preparation of the service. I've also included some sample eulogies.

The only way to learn fully is by doing. However, funerals require delicate, tactful, and deliberate performance and delivery. They provide one of the few times when people are forced to consider soberly the brevity of life and their need to face God. What a unique opportunity to proclaim God's love! Be as prepared as possible before your first call.

Postscript

Not long after this manuscript was accepted for publication, I encountered a funeral situation that easily held my swelling pride in check.

Without my knowledge a family scheduled a service at our church building. I became aware through various sources that several soloists and even a choir had been asked to participate. At the last minute I was asked to conduct the service.

It seemed as if the Lord was providing a test for me. After managing most of the complications associated with the service and even a few surprises, I felt almost proud of myself as the family slowly greeted one another outside the building and prepared to get into their cars for the seven-mile trip to the cemetery.

I felt confident and in charge as I entered the office to review a few last-minute things with the church secretary before the procession began.

The high ended for me abruptly. I walked out the door of the church building just in time to see the last car of the procession and the motorcycle escort drive away. I took several side streets, sweating profusely. The Lord rescued me again. I beat the procession by about three minutes.

Part 1

Preparing a Meaningful Funeral Service

1

Preparing Yourself

There is a time to be born and a time to die.

If you plan to preach or to be in the ministry, you can expect to be asked to officiate at funerals. Also, you can expect that many of those funerals will come at the most inopportune times. Especially during my younger years, people seemed inclined to die a day or two before I was scheduled to go on vacation with my family. To tell a grieving family to whom you are close that you will be unavailable for a service for their loved one is not easy to do.

There is another unique factor about funerals. If you set a speaking engagement, you generally allow time for preparation. But it is a rare funeral that you know about many days in advance. In the case of Jewish services, burial is almost immediate. However, in the Los Angeles area, where I live, it is not uncommon for mortuaries to delay the services five days or more following the death. Given your other duties and necessary preparation, even five days may not seem long enough. If you have a morbid fear of corpses or death, you have your own emotional preparation to add.

19

How do you as a minister prepare yourself for that in-evitable moment? It depends somewhat on how comfortable you feel in the presence of death. If your experience is no better than my first one, and you have never seen a corpse, this is the week, while you are reading this book, to see one. The sooner you face it the better. It's like the old saying: "If you have to swallow a frog, don't look at it too long."

If you want to be of consolation to grieving families, your own debilitating fears should be dealt with quickly. The best way to deal with them, I believe, is to call a local mortician, explain who you are, and ask him if he would help you by giving you a tour of his establishment. Chances are he'll be happy to help. He can show you what processes the body undergoes to prepare it for the service, such as embalming, cosmetology, and apparel. He can also show you how bodies are picked up from hospitals or other locations of death and explain what paperwork or arrangements may be necessary prior to his coming. In some cases, families may have to give written consent before a body can be released by a hospital to a mortuary. Also, the mortician can explain the types of services that are typically done in your area. Regional cus-toms differ substantially. Some of these differences will be discussed later.

A visit to the funeral home will help you overcome your fears. It can also enable you to reassure the families that you will counsel and serve later. They will have many questions and concerns. If you can explain things competently, they will have greater confidence in you.

You may also want to attend a few services conducted by your peers. You can observe the strengths and weaknesses of their presentations and note the formats they use.

The most effective preparation of all, however, is to read the Word. Acquaint yourself with the promises of the Lord in Scripture concerning death and resurrection. Examine the way Jesus confronted death. He prepared his disciples for the inevitability of his own death by prophesying it (see Matt. 16:21, 20:18, and others). Note, too, the emotion with which he prayed in the garden. Death stands against life. It is the "wages of sin." Even the Son of God faced it in anguish and apparent trepidation. I've always been wary of poets' easy platitudes.

Yet it is not a time for despair if one is in Christ. Jesus won victory over death by his resurrection. Among the richest resources of the Bible are passages assuring that victory. Among these are: Isaiah 25:6–8; John 5, 11, 14; 1 Corinthians 15; Romans 8; 1 Thessalonians 4, 5, and Revelation 7, 21, 22.

Before calling on a family, spend time in prayer. Tell God your fears. Ask for his wisdom and seek his consolation for the family.

It is possible that you have had long experience helping people through grief and you feel confident to help others face it. As I've gained experience, one hazard I've fallen victim to is being too sure of myself. My own overconfidence has led me at times to be insensitive to the pain of mourners. It is possible to be so clinical, professional, and experienced, that we are not humane. Remember, at the grave of Lazarus "Jesus wept."

2

Preparing for the Service

In Southern California, the greater number of funerals among the unchurched and Protestants is held in mortuary chapels. This is in contrast with many other parts of the country where most services are held in church buildings. I know of no spiritual reason why they should be held in church sanctuaries. I can think of many practical reasons for conducting them in mortuary chapels, especially in urban areas. In fact, it can be hazardous to drive in long processions through the streets of large cities from the service to the burial place. The mortuary facilities are usually better suited for funeral arrangements than are church buildings. However, we always try to accommodate any family that prefers to use our church building.

Mortuaries in the Southern California area offer a full range of services besides providing chapels. They arrange to have ministers, all kinds of musicians, and could presumably have a stand-up comic if the family desired.

Many urban and rural churches have musical groups that specialize in providing music for funerals of members. I generally try to follow the wishes of the family in respect to music. I couldn't say how many times I've heard "The Old Rugged Cross," but if it consoles the family it's okay with me.

I generally follow this format, which allows for variations:

Song (optional)
Obituary
Reading of Scripture
Prayer
Song
Eulogy
Song
Prayer (If there is a grave-side committal service, some
    families prefer not to have a closing prayer at the chapel
    or church, but prayer is always appropriate.)

Even though the family gives obituary information to the
funeral director or counselor, I try to obtain it from the family myself for several reasons. One of the most important is to
learn how to pronounce names of survivors (correct pronun-
ciation is crucial). Actually I regard every part of the service
as critical, because emotions are so tense. Second, typograph-
ical errors frequently are made by the funeral-home staff.
Don't depend on their correctness. A third reason to ask the
family is that it helps you to learn more about the deceased's
situation.

Even though I might have been with the family at the time
of death of their loved one, I try to make a separate appointment to talk about the service. It's good to let them know in
advance why you are coming so they can gather any information that might be helpful in preparing the eulogy.

When you meet with the family, get them to talk. Write
down everything you hear, even things that may not seem
too significant. Encourage them to reflect on their lives.

The session you have with the family serves another
important purpose. It helps you to understand their state of
mind and the particular needs you may have to address either
in the service or later.

What sort of information do you need and how do you
obtain it? To personalize the eulogy, you will need to famil-

iarize yourself with the personality of the deceased through the survivors' eyes. This can be difficult. In the first place, you may barely know the family, and second, the circumstances are far from normal. You may have to approach it from several different directions before you obtain what you need. It can require dogged persistence.

However, if you don't succeed in every case, don't feel that you have failed. There can be several reasons for failure, many of them not yours. I once spent more than an hour with a family for whom I had been asked to do a service. The father/husband had died. I met with the widow and two sons to get information for the service. As I tried to extract information, the conversation went something like this:

"Can you tell me something about your late husband's interests or hobbies?"

"He didn't have any. He just watched TV."

"Any special programs he liked?"

"No, he just watched everything."

"Can you tell me something about him that you remember best?"

"Nope. He was just an ordinary person."

Those people got an ordinary funeral. There was not much I could do about it.

I find it best to attempt to get the family comfortable with me first. It has been effective for me to briefly share some loss that I have experienced.

However, I believe it best not to say, "I know how you feel." Rather, you can share the pain and fear that you have experienced in similar circumstances. If you have never lost someone close to you, this is a little more difficult. But it is perfectly appropriate to say something like, "I know that what you are feeling right now must be very painful. Would it help to talk about it?"

The griever might say no. In that case you can suggest that you would like to talk later when the griever feels better. Tactfully explain that it will help you to conduct a more meaningful service if the family can tell you a little about the one they have lost.

Most people are willing to talk. Often there are relatives present who are helpful. They are often comfortable speaking to the griever, and you can take notes of their conversations. There is a long list of sayings that well-intentioned people launch onto grieving people. When one of my sisters died about twenty years ago, I must have heard every trite saying there is, such as "God knows what is best." Not one of them helped, and in some cases they got under my skin.

When Job's friends went to console him they did the right thing for the first seven days. They didn't say a word. But once they started talking they were of no more help than his nagging wife. A warm handshake, or a hug if you are familiar with the person, will express your love and concern better than any words. It is always appropriate to say that you will pray for the family. If they are believers (church members) you will not hesitate to say a prayer with them. If they are not members and you don't know their status, I think it is wise to ask if they would like to have you pray with them.

One way to get the family to talk about the deceased is to be alert to photos and evidence of hobbies and interests in the home and to ask about them. You can ask about specific incidents or outings such as fishing trips or travel. You may focus on church work or activity in volunteer organizations, or the deceased's relationship with his/her children or grandchildren.

I recently met with a family that had lost a mother/ grandmother. As they began to reminisce, they laughed about her Brooklyn accent and the way she pronounced certain words. They also spoke of the appetite for pizza that she developed in later life. I made reference to both in the service. A little humor adds realism and also breaks the heavy tension that pervades so many funerals. Every human being has foibles, and if the family makes reference to them, I usually take the liberty to make some comment. I do not refer to major difficulties such as problems with alcohol or mental illness, but if a person tended to be short tempered, it's a little ridiculous to say how much he or she loved everyone.

Several years ago a neighbor friend of ours died. He had owned and operated a small business in our community. At the service, the rabbi, who incidentally didn't know him, spoke about how the deceased had loved and respected everyone who came into his shop. When I had coffee with the store owner's son about a week after the funeral to see how he was adjusting, we spoke about the service. He noted that there were a few times he wanted to go check the coffin to make sure it was his dad the rabbi was talking about. His father definitely did not like everyone who came into his shop. In fact, he had tossed several people out. The son felt that the inaccurate comments had made the service seem unreal.

Be sure to take a note pad or a good supply of 4" x 6" cards. As you listen to the family reminisce and give you information, write down everything that is said. (I prefer to use 4" x 6" cards or smaller pieces of paper so that in the office when I prepare the eulogy I can see all the information before me instead of having to turn sheets of paper back and forth. One other timesaving idea I've learned is to check off in my rough notes or strike through information as I use it so I'm not repeating material already used.) Most family members commenting on the deceased will say, "She was a wonderful mother" or "I couldn't have asked for a better father." I try to be as faithful as my conscience will allow to the information given me. However, I believe it's wise to avoid overuse of superlatives. Too many "bests" and "greatests" can cause your comments to lose credibility.

Why do I so carefully gather this information? I believe it is important to personalize funerals as much as possible. One of the benefits is that it helps to induce weeping, thereby nurturing the grieving process. I attempt to do this by drawing a picture of the deceased as he or she was in life so that certain events and memories can be relived by the mourners. In another chapter I have included some sample services so you can see how I do it. It is not the only way, and I cannot claim that it is the best way, but it has been helpful to me.

I have established some principles for myself. First, I don't attempt to relegate anyone to hell or install anyone in the heavenly realms. As Paul said, "The sins of some men are conspicuous, pointing to judgment, but the sins of others appear later" (1 Tim. 5:24 RSV).

Once I went to the home of a man who had been active in our church to talk to his widow about funeral arrangements. She warned me about saying good things about him. He was one of those who for years had fooled everyone but his wife and a few neighbors. As far as I know, no one in the church ever suspected he had a severe problem with gambling and other assorted vices. I surely had not.

It is always helpful to speak of specific things the deceased has done, just as the widows who showed "tunics and other garments which Dorcas made while she was with them" (Acts 9:39 RSV). But to assign a heavenly berth or a cubicle of hell is not wise to do. I can't say for sure that anyone will be in heaven; only the Lord truly knows who are his. However, I can relate the person's witness of his or her faith.

In every instance, I try to accomplish the following without fail:

1. Help mourners come to terms with death. This is done by the use of Scripture that reminds us of the brevity of life. Poetry and quotations of people who have learned to recognize this are very helpful—the more contemporary the source, the better. Mourners must be brought to the "brink of the grave" and encouraged to face the horrible reality of death, not to practice denial.

2. Induce mourning. Draw verbal pictures of the life and activities of the deceased. On numerous occasions, I have asked personal friends of the deceased to help do this by speaking for three to five minutes. I tell them specifically what I would like them to do and how much time they should take. I've never had anyone abuse the opportunity.

3. Deal with guilt. Guilt will be felt to some extent by all the mourners. Urge them to confess it to God—according to 1 John 1:9. Tell them of the guilt you have felt in various circumstances and how good it feels to be forgiven in Christ.

4. Encourage active participation by the mourners. If the mourners listen to a solo or organist and hear readings, prayers, and a eulogy by you, their experience will be entirely passive. Their active participation will enhance their ability to deal with their grief. How can you actively involve the mourners? Use responsive readings or have them recite a familiar psalm with you. Encourage congregational singing. In the case of small gatherings, you can encourage each of the mourners to relate some experiences (see chapter on alternative services).

5. Present living hope in Christ. I generally introduce this by saying something like the following:

"How can we prepare ourselves for times like today? We need to have our own lives in readiness.

"How is this done? We must come to terms with who Jesus is. He was not just another man, not just a good teacher or philosopher. He was sent from God and is uniquely God's son.

"He lived a perfect life that accomplished at least two things. First, by his example he demonstrated the content of a perfect life of love, humility, courage, purity, and faithfulness to God. Second, he successfully resisted all temptation. He was tempted in all ways, as we are, yet he did not sin (see Heb. 4:15).

"When Jesus was executed it was for our failures, not his. He paid the penalty we deserve."

I then briefly explain the heart of the good news about Jesus, using the basic points in the sermons found in the Book of Acts: (1) God sent Jesus into the world; (2) we crucified him; (3) God raised him on the third day; (4) He ascended to the right hand of God; (5) salvation is only in him; (6) he will return to judge the world by his righteousness.

I also explain how we can share in his resurrection if we are in him. I rely heavily on the following passages: 1 Corinthians 15, 2 Corinthians 5, 1 Thessalonians 4:13–18. I recall how impressed a nonbelieving medical doctor was at the reading from 1 Corinthians 15 during a service for his wife, who was a believer. His rational mind was deeply convicted by the proofs of Jesus' resurrection that Paul delineates in the first several verses. As I read Paul's reminder that more than five hundred witnesses, most of whom were still alive at his writing, had seen Jesus at once, I could hear the old doctor say to his son, "I like that."

The message about Jesus is convicting. It is life.

3

When You Are the Bearer of Bad News

On some occasions it will be your unenviable responsibility to inform the family of the death of one of their members. Few occasions require more prayerful tact and wisdom and greater sensitivity.

Not long ago, I had to call the daughter of an old friend to tell her that I had found her father dead on the floor of his apartment. The daughter lived out of state. When I called her, my first words were: "I've got some bad news for you." She could tell from the tone of my voice what the bad news was and queried me further about the details. In her case, I knew her family well and was confident of her ability to handle the information by herself. If the family were within driving distance, I would not phone but simply go directly to the home of the survivors to tell them in person.

When You Tell Them

Should they be standing or sitting when you tell them? It's best to have them sit and then give them the information in as tender, straightforward terms as you can. Some people will possibly faint or collapse at the news. If they are sitting, there is far less likelihood of injury.

Many, however, will get up immediately and start to pace nervously about. If you have experienced the death of a loved one, you know the numbing sensation that sets in immediately. The news is too horrible to accept in one course, and your mind and body begin the long process of acceptance that has been so well described by Elisabeth Kübler-Ross and others. Because of fear and shock there will be great surges of adrenalin, and yet some motor functions may be impaired.

It is my opinion that mourners should be encouraged to weep as much as possible. Walk with them to help them work off some of the pent-up energy. It is far healthier to weep openly and expressively than to maintain a public stoicism. Those who weep will get past the grief process far more effectively and completely.

Though I run the risk of being at odds with some in the medical profession, neither do I believe that tranquilizers are healthy. The Lord made the processes of grief that have been effective for thousands of years. The use of tranquilizers only suppresses or retards the natural process.

Let's say that sister A and sister B lose a brother. Sister A reacts by screaming and crying out "No! No!" for several minutes, then continues to sob almost convulsively for hours.

Sister B, on the other hand, accepts the news quietly and sits misty eyed for a time, but soon joins with others in consoling sister A. Which sister is doing better? If you asked most people, they would say sister B is handling the situation well. Generalizations can be dangerous, because no two people ever react the same way to any news, good or bad. But I believe that sister A, if she continues to express her grief, will adjust better because she has not withheld or suppressed it.

Women can often handle grief much more effectively than men, because there are fewer social or cultural restrictions against public demonstrations of weeping by women. Both in

counseling families on the day of the death of a loved one
and at funerals, too, I encourage weeping as much as possible.

How do you encourage people to cry?

First, you give permission by telling them it's all right, perfectly natural to weep. Second, you induce weeping by talking as much as possible about their lost loved one.

If you knew the deceased, you can speak of your recollections and attempt to converse with the family to encourage
their reflection. If you did not know the deceased, you can
simply say, "Tell me something about your sister. What do
you remember best about her?"

If you knew the deceased, it is helpful to relate experiences
that you shared. In Acts 9:36, Tabitha (Dorcas) has just died.
She had been an extraordinary woman, "who was always
doing good and helping the poor." Her loved ones had
washed her body and were weeping over it. When Peter
arrived "he was taken upstairs to the room. All the widows
stood around him, crying and showing him the robes and
other clothing that Dorcas had made while she was still with
them."

What the widows did enabled the grief process. The clothing they displayed helped them to remember Dorcas and her
good deeds. Possibly one said, "Dorcas made this gown for
me last month when I was sick." Another would say, "Just
after my husband died, Dorcas brought me this beautiful
tunic she had made."

It helps to recollect the good deeds of the deceased. "He
used to drive me to the doctor," or "She volunteered several
hours a week to feed the hungry people on Main Street. I
recall what joy it brought her to serve."

However, don't talk too much and don't talk too soon.
When loved ones are first told they may just need a good
shoulder to cry on for a while. Let them cry as long as they
like. If the grieving person is young, and you are young (or
even old) and of the opposite sex, it's a good idea to have
someone else with you. If it is a woman you are visiting, and
you are a man, take one or more of the sisters from the

church to be in the home with you. Emotions are extremely complex. Fires of passion can be aroused in times of grief. This is not the time to get life more complicated for you or the griever.

Don't try to minimize the importance of the loved ones' loss and don't offer clichés about it being God's will. In fact, it is probably wisest to keep advice to an absolute minimum. Simply be a quiet, concerned friend.

What is appropriate to say? Brief readings of Scripture are always the best counsel. Psalms 23 or 91 and 1 Corinthians 15 are very helpful. You can pray with them, helping them to verbalize the pain they feel. It is good for them to honestly express their pain.

David was famous for telling God of his anger and disappointment. Psalm 60 begins with his typical honest frustration: "You have rejected us, O God, and burst forth upon us; you have been angry—now restore us!"

One way to assist grievers toward honest expression is by your own honesty. Tell of your pain in a similar circumstance. You may want to take mental notes, if not paper-and-pencil notes, of what is said so it can be dealt with at more length later and to make sure that all the bitterness eventually gets worked through.

How do you determine when it is appropriate for you to leave? You will have to use your judgment based on the answers to some simple questions. Does the griever agree with the idea when you say you are about to leave? Are there family members or church members or close friends present who can assist when you depart? Has the griever worked through the initial highly emotional reaction? Those who stay should be advised that the best therapy is S.A.S. (sit and be silent) so the griever will have time to reflect and sob.

Thinking About Details

Usually the family needs help in several ways. Relatives should be notified. The grief sitter can ask, "Would you like some help in calling your loved ones?" After getting a note pad the griever can help list the names and tell where the numbers can be found.

Funeral arrangements should be made. Has the deceased made prior arrangements? If so, where are the instructions? Has a mortuary been selected? It would be wise for you as a minister to know of a couple of reputable firms to which grievers can be referred. If you give them the names of two or more, you will be above possible accusations of collusion with the mortuary. It is good for someone to go to the mortuary with the griever.

In the case of large families, accommodating visiting mourners can be a real but necessary chore. A concerned but organized friend should be identified who can coordinate arrangements for out-of-town relatives, meet them at the airport, and find lodging for them while they are in town.

The family will need help immediately in other ways, too. The process of grieving requires great energy. The mind is so busy grappling with the ugliness of death, attempting to accept it, and coming to terms with it, that there can be little physical energy left. Grievers are often disorganized, disoriented, and unable to plan the smallest of tasks. Church members can render a good ministry in the grief process by assisting with dishes, cooking meals, cleaning house, answering the door, and calling relatives. Obviously, the privacy of the mourners must be respected. However, the above are areas where mourners are often happy to receive help. There will be some who will prefer to handle all matters by themselves, and their needs should be tactfully respected.

In rural communities, traditions have often been established so that help has been given to the mourners in the same way for generations. Urban communities often lack these traditions, but the church or other organizations can fill a needed role. You can do yourself and your church an important service by setting some systems in place to be ready when they are needed.

If you are new in your community, it would be wise to talk with some of the old-timers to discover what the local traditions are. In some communities wakes are still a standard practice.

To know what your resources are for transportation, food, assistance with housework, etc., it might be wise to encourage your deacons to conduct a survey of your church members. It will assist you to identify those that can be called in time of need.

Just today I spoke with a Catholic woman in her early forties whose mother died suddenly. They had lived together for many years. The mother did not answer the phone when the daughter called from work to find out how she was doing. The daughter went to the house and found her mother dead on the floor. When she called her church, no priest was available, but the parish sent a woman, a volunteer experienced in dealing with situations like the one my friend was undergoing. This volunteer performed a good ministry. It is very helpful to have a group of volunteers who can be mobilized to deal with circumstances of grief.

Dealing with Guilt

One of the strongest emotions connected with death is guilt. It is almost universally expressed. Guilt is felt even where the relationships have been good and wholesome. It is the nature of human beings to leave things unsaid and undone. There are matters you intend to discuss with your spouse but haven't yet brought up. You intend to do things with or for your spouse that you haven't done. If your spouse dies with these things unresolved, it poses a real dilemma. It leaves you unable to make amends. Husbands and wives leave the house in the morning having had harsh words with their spouses. Sometimes they don't return. When they don't, it leaves the survivor with a crushing load of guilt.

In 1966, there was a series of deaths of persons close to me. In the case of each one there was unresolved guilt. That guilt exacerbated other inadequacies I felt at the time. It took several months for me to work through it. It would have been much easier had someone explained to me that it is normal to feel that way.

It is necessary to explain how normal the presence of guilt is. It is also important to provide some means of coping with it realistically. Frequently counselors will tell grievers not to worry about guilt. That doesn't make the guilt go away. They need to feel forgiven by the Lord. 1 John 1:9, "If we confess our sins, he is faithful and just and will forgive us our sins and purify us from all unrighteousness," has been of great consolation to me. Help mourners to verbalize their feelings to the Lord and to ask his forgiveness.

Dealing with Children

What do you say to children? It's best, I believe, to keep children informed. Tell them honestly and answer their questions in a simple, straightforward manner. I don't think we should try to hide things from them. They sense things. They also have vivid imaginations.

Some years ago I met a family at a funeral home. The grandmother had died, and the family had gathered to view her remains in the "slumber room." Her daughter was the mother of a girl of about five years old. The family was preparing to go to the slumber room, and the little girl wanted to go along. The mother didn't want her to go. She believed that little children should not be exposed to death. I encouraged her to take the child with her. What the child imagined about death—what was in that mysterious room about which everyone spoke in whispers—would have been far worse than anything the child actually saw. There was no evidence that she suffered any from the experience. It was quite the contrary.

When our children were small, they attended funerals with us. Children are far more apt to verbalize their fears than adults. When they do you can address them. When our four children were between the ages of four and ten, one of their cousins died of sudden infant death syndrome at eighteen months. It was a difficult night for our youngsters. They remembered having seen the little boy the summer before on our vacation. Our ten-year-old son was the most upset.

As I began talking with him I recognized that his greatest fear was for his cousin's fate. When I explained to him that no little child who dies will ever leave God's care, that God loves them, and that they will be in heaven with him, he stopped his sobbing and in just a short time fell asleep.

To be honest, if I did not believe that, I don't know what I would or could say to children or adults.

Leaving Grievers Alone

Should the griever be left to himself or herself? I believe that in most cases space and time should be provided for grievers to be alone. They need time to work through their loss. They should be advised to reflect quietly on the one they have lost, to try to remember good times and bad times. They may relive certain incidents again and again. It is not morbid. Instead, this is the natural process for coming to terms with the loss. Again, it would be helpful to identify in advance within your church family persons willing to volunteer for one or all of the above. They should be trained adequately and be on call for their services.

The three exceptions are the following who should not be left alone:

1. Minors. The first thing to do is to get legal counsel if minors within your church family have been orphaned. If you have had no experience in this area, be sure to consult a trustworthy person who has and whom you should identify now.

2. Suicidal persons. How do you know if a person is suicidal? If that person is reputed to be or has talked of it, you are well advised to consult a fully trained counselor. Be especially wary if the person has indicated to you what method of suicide he or she intends to use—knife, razor blades, gas, etc. If persons have thought about it to the point that they have considered a means, take the threat especially seriously.

3. Infirm or extremely elderly people. Several persons have consulted me recently on dealing with their mates who have

Alzheimer's disease. Their concern is that if they should die first, who will help care for the surviving spouse who is afflicted with Alzheimer's. It is important to have written instructions beforehand and to proceed with legal counsel. Obtain clarification and accord of the family members. Files containing instructions and whom to call can be placed for easy access in the church office.

One Final Important Point

Do not necessarily assume that you will be the officiant at the funeral. Sometimes the family has an old friend or a favorite uncle or aunt or a son-in-law who is a minister, and they may have already made a commitment to have that person officiate.

The best way to clarify it is to state sincerely that you will be glad to help in any way you can. Usually at that point they will ask you to do the service. Then you can make an appointment with them to return and discuss the arrangements.

In the event they do not respond by clarifying their intentions, you can ask something like the following: "Have you made arrangements for a minister to officiate, or would you like for me to help you?"

Before you leave the home, pray with the mourners, if they consent, and set an appointment for a time mutually convenient when you can return to discuss funeral arrangements.

4

Legal Questions and Mortuaries

Some of the nastiest and most perplexing problems surrounding death are the legal and financial questions that arise. Two of the most difficult legal questions have to do with autopsies and embalming. Because laws vary from state to state, you will have to investigate which laws apply locally. In California presently, if a person has not seen a physician for a prescribed length of time, an autopsy is required. Contrary to some popular myths, an autopsy does not require total dismemberment or disfigurement of the body. In fact, most of the time no layman would ever see that an autopsy had been performed.

In certain cases, hospitals may want to perform them for different reasons, some having to do with medical advancement and training, but they usually obtain family permission.

Some years ago, a little boy about six years old, whose family attended our church, developed a virulent form of cancer. He was hospitalized in one of the facilities in Los Angeles that treats children. The family had limited income and probably was charged very little if any for several weeks of medical inpatient treatment at the hospital. When the little boy died, the medical staff at the hospital put tremendous pressure on the mother to allow an autopsy on the child. Though I felt bad for the people at the hospital who would benefit from the training, their approach to the mother was causing her so much stress that I helped her resist the pressure.

The family may get pressure from another source. In this case it is very subtle, but for that reason it can be even more difficult to resist. A family may shift from being very angry with doctors or others they feel are connected with their loved one's death to feeling overwhelming guilt. One way to "make up" for wrongs done to or neglect of the departed one is to have a "nice funeral." Guilt makes people susceptible to doing things they would never do without its pressure.

A casket cannot help a corpse. A corpse can't feel, sense, see, smell, or hear anything. It will, in a fairly short time, be dust. But that logic rarely prevails in the purchase of the casket unless saner heads have prevailed prior to the death. Most mortuaries are operated, I believe, by basically honest people. It is true that most morticians do not stand over you insisting that you purchase their deluxe models of copper caskets supplied with inner spring mattresses, satin, lace, and double sealed liners to keep out the elements. It's also true that they don't twist your arm to sell you the lot that is under the shady oak tree or at the top of the hill having a view of the whole valley. But what they tend to do is to show you the expensive models and lots first. After you have seen the deluxe ones, you are shown the less expensive ones. They are drab in contrast. Remember that guilt? "Nothing is too good for our mother!"

Imagine going to an auto showroom where in the most prominent, visible location are expensive Rolls-Royces, Mercedes, and other luxury cars. After you have admired these, you are shown several rows of sports cars, then mid-sized cars. Far in the back, almost in the dark area, are a few economy models. Supposing you had promised your mother you would buy her a car, and she went to the showroom with you. Even if you could afford nothing but the cheapest economy model, you would still probably feel like a cheapskate after you had seen the Rolls-Royce and Mercedes-Benz models. That's part of the pressure you are under in the casket selection room.

A friend of ours of modest income who attends another church recently lost her mother. She called asking my advice on the selection of a funeral home. I gave her the names of a couple of mortuaries and also forewarned her about the sales techniques she would be subject to. She thanked me for the advice because, as she expressed it, she was afraid she would be taken advantage of and she wanted my assistance in resisting the pressures. I was satisfied that she understood the warnings and precautions I advised.

At the funeral service I was amazed to see that she had selected one of the most expensive caskets available for her mother. Where did I fail? I still don't know.

In other cases I have been somewhat more successful but have paid a price. I mentioned earlier that I was on call for two of the largest mortuaries in Southern California to do services for persons who desired a Church of Christ minister but who were not members of a particular congregation. I also did services at those mortuaries for other persons who had no church background. The family simply requested a minister, and the mortuary arranged for me to come.

All of that came to an end several years ago when a member of our church, a grandmother in her seventies, died. The woman's daughter was in failing health. The granddaughters had to make arrangements for the funeral. They were in their early twenties, had little business experience and no experience in arranging for funerals. They asked me to accompany them.

After all the information had been obtained by the counselor, it was time to go to the casket selection room. On entering the room we were greeted by the presence of all those luxury models I have described. The daughters immediately fell in love with one. Its cost was several thousand dollars. I suggested that it might be wise to look a little further. They agreed. The counselor was becoming exasperated by the potential loss of commission, but told the young women he would step outside so they would be free to choose whatever casket they wished.

After he was gone, I asked the young women about their ability to pay for the casket. They were of limited income and would have had to finance a great share of the cost. I suggested to them that the casket would not help their grandmother. It would be buried, and their only reminder would be a long series of payments. They finally agreed on a moderately priced casket that was considerably narrower than the one they had originally admired. The new casket was still more expensive than they could afford, but given their state of mind I doubted whether they could have accepted a cheaper looking casket.

When the counselor reappeared, he was visibly chagrined by their choice. Not yet having given up on his possible loss of commission he approached the casket they had chosen, remarking, "The choice is entirely yours, of course, but remember (at that moment he drew a tape measure out of his pocket and started measuring the inside width of the casket) your grandmother is a woman of considerable girth. I'm not sure she will fit in this casket." With that comment I drew him aside and insisted, "I'm sure you can squeeze her in." They did. The mortuary stopped calling me to do services after that.

If you know that the family is of limited income and no previous arrangements have been made, you may want to accompany the surviving family members to help them to survive financially. But another precaution: you don't want to increase the family's stress by causing a conflict with the mortician.

The answer may well be to have some class sessions for church members on dealing with funeral arrangements and money management.

Is it necessary to embalm? At present in California it is not necessary if burial takes place within the state. However, for shipment out of state for burial, corpses must be embalmed.

What is embalming? It consists mostly of draining blood and pumping a preservative solution through the veins.

The family will encounter many other choices. These will include whether to purchase flowers to cover the casket and how much should be spent for them; whether to have flowers present in the room where the corpse reposes prior to the funeral; whether to have limousine service; whether a vault is necessary and what type of interment there will be.

Because caskets will eventually collapse, causing the lawn surface to sink, some cemeteries require a concrete liner or vault for the casket's exterior. These come in high- and low-priced models. Be aware that morticians speak of "protection"—protection for a body that will never feel a thing again and will eventually be dust.

What about cremation? Cremation was once the choice of a few persons noted for their idiosyncracies. It is becoming increasingly popular, definitely not the emotional issue it once was. Cremation saves expenses of burial and real estate, and also in some cases saves expense of the casket. Some people I've talked with worry about the loss of the body for resurrection purposes. In my opinion it is no more difficult for the Lord to raise a body which has been consumed by fire than it is for him to raise a body which has been dead five days. All things are possible for him.

5

Terminal Illness
and Predeath Situations

One of the most telling factors in the way we handle grief is the manner in which we prepare for it. It is somewhat like preparing for retirement. Some people don't want to think about it until the day it takes place, and they are totally unprepared.

There are many middle-aged people in our country whose parents have been confined for years in convalescent homes. Many of them will be no better prepared for their parents' deaths than a Midwesterner is for a tidal wave.

Two areas of concern will be treated in this chapter. First, should a dying person be told that he will die? Second, how does the family prepare when one of its members has a terminal illness?

The first question deals with a many-sided issue. Occasionally, medical societies and other special-interest groups hold seminars on the subject. It would be helpful to take advantage of these opportunities.

A number of years ago, I was trapped in a nasty dilemma while dealing with the stepfather of an old school friend. He had cancer, but for some reason the physician had never told him how serious it was. His wife asked me to visit him, which I did almost weekly for several months in their home. His condition progressively worsened, but he always spoke of recovery.

One day the wife walked me to the door and begged me to help her. Her husband had never made out a will, which meant at that time in California that the estate would be tied up in probate unless he did something about it. His physician, however, had ordered that he not be informed that his condition was terminal. His doctor was probably one of those few persons unable to come to terms with death himself.

The wife was afraid to disobey the doctor's order, but at the same time seemed to be in jeopardy of substantial financial loss were the husband to die without preparing a will. My naiveté and inexperience left me very insecure in that situation. After agonizing over the question for a long time I finally sought help from my physician and an attorney friend.

We arrived at this solution. Instead of singling out just the dying husband I was to speak to the two of them together, pointing out that in view of their age it was important that they have wills prepared to make sure their wishes would be carried out. The husband did query me as to why I brought up the subject, but I was able to respond with all sincerity that both of them needed to have their affairs in order because of their age.

As it turned out, the deed had already been prepared so that it was not a problem for the wife. However, she had had no way of knowing it prior to the conversation.

Is it wise to tell a person that his or her condition is terminal? There are strong arguments on both sides. I believe the dying should be told of the seriousness of their condition. They need to have frank, open discussions with their loved ones. The family members need also to resolve any conflicts they may have had with the patient.

On the other hand, who can state with certainty when death will come? About twenty-three years ago, my niece was suffering from a rare childhood disease. Doctors had given her only a few months to live. She lived in the Pacific Northwest. One of my sisters, the girl's aunt, thought it would be a great idea to bring our niece to Los Angeles and take her to Disneyland so she could have one last wish before she died. I remember accompanying them. It was hardly a happy time for us. I fought back tears, convinced that I was seeing her alive for the last time.

There was a death within the next several months, but it was not my niece's. It was my sister's—the one who had arranged the Disneyland trip for our niece. And my niece, how is she doing? I had the honor of performing her wedding ceremony a few years ago in Portland. She and her husband now have a child of their own.

Another point to consider is that it is possible to destroy one's will to live by telling him with too much certainty what his prognosis is. In each instance it is a question to which doctors, family, and ministers should give much prayer and carefully weigh the individual circumstances.

How do you prepare a family when the death of a loved one is reasonably certain or near? It is, I believe, necessary to first broach the subject by asking a question like, "Have you considered what life will be like when _____ is not here?" The reaction to that question will give you clues as to how to proceed. Tears may come to their eyes, or you might get a response such as, "I don't want to think about it!"

It would be helpful for you to relate your own fears. This will enable family members to open up to you so you can identify what their real anxieties are. In some cases you may fail to accomplish this. You may hint, suggest, or even talk bluntly to no avail. Some people absolutely refuse to think about death. If you have made a thoughtful, loving, prayerful attempt and don't succeed, don't blame yourself too harshly. It is not easy to undo years of conditioning.

I have left the most important thing until last. No person should ever be in our presence very long without hearing the comforting, consoling message of good news about Jesus. It's the greatest help of all in every circumstance.

In the case of my friend's father, I may have been successful in dealing with his wife's legal-financial problem, but I hardly dealt with the greater issue of death at all. To be sure, all of us have a responsibility to free our loved ones from legal complications by leaving our houses in order. But there is a larger and greater issue. Why didn't my friend's father know, or admit that he knew (if he did know), that he was dying? Some of us don't know too much; yet there is one thing that we should know: our own bodies.

If we have been told that we have cancer involving some vital organ, and if that organ should be so adversely affected that bodily functions are seriously impaired, it ought to be a sure clue that we may have a limited number of days. It seems to me that we should know our bodies well enough to have some understanding or inkling of the seriousness of the problem we face. What I'm suggesting is that the evidence should have been overwhelming to my friend's father that he was dying. Yet for some reason he missed or avoided all the clues. Was it because he sensed everyone else was avoiding it, too, so that he couldn't bring himself to the point of openly discussing a subject that was frightening everyone else? It is quite possible that the condition was created just as much by the dread expressed, albeit nonverbally, by the family, the doctor, and me as by the dying man's fear.

Actually, many dying persons are able to come to terms with their conditions and carry on frank, open discussions with those close to them. Some of the most candid, intriguing discussions I've ever had were with two different friends—one who was dying from leukemia and the other from Lou Gehrig's disease (amyotrophic lateral sclerosis).

It will be of great help to the family later, as well as immediately helpful to the terminally ill person, if candid conversations can be encouraged. Members of the family can speak about their love and appreciation for their loved ones. They may eventually become comfortable enough to clear up any misunderstandings that may have existed. And it lets the dying person know he or she is not dying alone. A minister is in a unique position to guide a family in this.

6

Grave-Side Services

It is customary to conclude a service at the place of interment. This may be at the grave side, mausoleum, or niche where ashes are placed.

Usually there is a cortege, that is, an auto procession, although at some cemeteries in which funeral services are held in chapels on the grounds you may simply walk to the place of interment.

At the close of the service it takes the mortuary personnel a few minutes to remove the flowers, transport them to the cemetery, and place them at the grave side. Funeral directors like to have the flowers placed before the family arrives. You can use the time to ready your notes and read over the Scriptures you plan to use at the committal service. If you are unfamiliar with the mortuary, ask the director out of which door they will take the casket. You don't want to be standing by yourself in front of the chapel while they are loading the hearse in the rear.

When the mortician has everything ready he will wheel the casket toward the exit where the pallbearers are waiting. Or the pallbearers may carry or escort it from its resting place in the chapel. Customs on this vary from place to place. You should walk a few paces in front of the casket until you reach the funeral coach (hearse). Stand out of the way facing the casket until it is placed in the coach and then return to your car.

In some parts of the country it is customary for the mourners to follow the casket from the church building or mortuary. Check with mortuary personnel or an older minister in your area to determine local customs.

Most directors will arrange for the minister to have a prominent place in the cortege. I've noticed that many younger directors are less attentive to detail, so possibly no one will reserve a place in the cortege for you. Should you insist on it? If you feel that it is important to you, do it. However, I feel the Lord has called me to be a servant, so if I'm not given a prominent position, I go to the back of the procession. If you are disabled or if the time element is crucial, explain it to the director ahead of time.

When you arrive at the place of interment you can, as soon as you park your car, go quickly to the rear of the funeral coach and stand in attendance until the casket is removed by the pallbearers. Be sure to ask the director ahead of time to point out the correct grave site and which route the procession will take. You will feel a little stupid heading toward the wrong open grave. Also ask which direction the casket will face. As you lead the procession to the grave it is wise to look back occasionally to see if they are keeping pace or are about to bump into you.

When you arrive at the grave site, stand at the foot of the grave, giving ample room for the pallbearers to place the casket. I've also learned that it's a good idea to watch the pallbearers carefully. The footing is often treacherous around a grave, and they are carrying a heavy load. Occasionally you may have to give assistance.

Usually the director will signal you when it is time to begin, when everything is in readiness. It generally takes a while for all the mourners to assemble. I have found it helpful to get myself ready then by praying quietly and reflecting on how I will begin.

It is often necessary to request people to gather in closer.

Remember, you will not have the benefit of a public address system, and there will be various outside noises including wind, rain, and airplanes. Use your strongest voice. To be sure you will be heard, you can ask someone (not a member of the immediate family) to stand toward the back and signal to you whether your voice volume is adequate.

If there has already been a service at the mortuary or church building, I usually read a few Scripture passages, recite or read an appropriate poem, and then have a concluding prayer.

If there has been no service at the chapel, you will likely want to give a brief eulogy. (Sample prayers, readings, and eulogies are given in chapter 10.)

Grave-side committal services most often end with prayer. When you have concluded, nod to the director, step to the foot of the casket if you are not already there, and the director will take over. Customs vary. Some people sprinkle soil on the casket and say, "Dust thou art. . . ." In other localities the casket is buried completely before the family leaves. In some areas it is customary for the pallbearers to place their boutonnières on the casket. The director will take care of this ceremony. If the deceased was a veteran, an American flag will often be draped over the casket. At the close of the service the director will fold the flag and hand it to a family member. As soon as these ceremonies are over, it is appropriate for you to walk over to where the family is sitting or standing and offer a firm handshake or a hug, depending on your familiarity with them. The mourners can then offer their condolences to the family.

How long should you stay at the grave side? This depends on how well you know the family, what their needs are, and your own schedule. If you are close to the family and they have few friends or no one else to give support, you may want to stay. If you have simply been "hired" by the mortuary to do the service, ask the immediate survivors if you can help in any way. Usually they will say no.

In some cases family members or friends will have a meal or gathering at the home or church hall of the deceased or a family member. The type of gathering can range from very solemn to very wild and raucous depending on the culture or family. If they invite you, it is proper to go, but do not be the last to leave. You must be the judge of how your time is spent. If I believe I can be of assistance to the mourners by my presence, or if I have an opportunity to declare my faith in Jesus, I will go. My decision obviously also depends on my schedule. Many times I have gone directly from a funeral to a wedding.

Before I leave I always ask the immediate survivors if I can be of further assistance. At times they will have questions. You can make a follow-up appointment in a few days. Keep your promise if you say you will call. You will experience a range of responses when you do call back. These will be discussed in chapter 9.

I believe that one of the greatest services you can render is to be observant of other family members who have special needs. At times a child will be especially baffled and pained by what is going on. Children have many questions, and often adults don't see their needs because of their own grief. If you see someone standing quietly off to one side, you are likely seeing someone in great need. You may be the right one to minister to such persons.

7

Alternative Services

Funerals are very expensive. They are also a custom which many people do not want to follow. What can you do in the event you are dealing with a family whose wishes differ from the norm, whether from financial need or not?

I believe that some of the nontraditional forms of services can be among the most helpful. I dealt with a family in the community not long ago who had lost a grandfather. He had not wanted a funeral. Yet there was a need for the family somehow to deal with their grief, and they asked for my help.

We arranged to have a family gathering. The wife and daughter, the son-in-law, the granddaughters and their husbands all met with me in the daughter's home one evening. (The grandfather's body already had been cremated.) I read a few Scripture passages and then asked each of the family members to share their best recollections of the deceased. We were sitting in a circle in the living room, and each shared in turn some event or memorable time. They laughed and cried and laughed and cried some more. After all had an opportunity for sharing, we closed with a prayer together. I think it was one of the most meaningful services I ever did, and I said so to that family.

A couple in their late thirties who attended our church several years ago looked forward to the birth of their first child. The baby boy was stillborn and his infant body cremated. The parents wanted to have a little service for him, but could not afford a funeral. We drove to a spot on a hillside overlooking the city. After I said a few words of consolation and prayed with them, they scattered the ashes and flowers down the hillside. It was one of the saddest occasions of my life and, obviously, very different from any other funeral service.

In some areas there is a growing custom to have a private burial service at the cemetery with only immediate family members present. Later (that evening or a day or two following the burial) a memorial (or victory celebration) service is held in the deceased's church.

When deciding alternatives to traditional services, the questions I ask myself are first, is it biblical, and second, is it legal? What does the family really want? Does this violate my conscience or compromise my beliefs in any way? Will what I do help them to grieve and to come to greater faith in God?

Having answered these questions I don't worry a lot about convention and custom.

8

Helpful Hints
for the Day of the Funeral

Be Prepared

Your confidence will be enhanced on the day of the funeral if you have finished your preparation for the service the day before. I occasionally extemporize talks but never a eulogy. I write out all the details and words. Perhaps after some years you will feel more confident than I do, but feelings are too sensitive and the atmosphere too heavy with emotion for mistakes. Gravediggers may cover the body afterward, but you will have a difficult time "covering" mistakes due to lack of preparation. Besides preparing your own part, make sure soloists, organists, and others know at what time of the service they will be needed.

Review

Review your notes of order of service and eulogy before you go to the service and once you arrive. Try to have the outline and what you will be doing firmly in your mind.

Be Early

I try to be at the place of service at least twenty minutes in advance. At times the family has last-minute requests, or you may need to clarify certain items. Sometimes they will recall an incident about Aunt Jane when she was twelve years old that they want mentioned. Or, they will recall that Uncle Charlie's favorite Scripture was Psalm 23. Early arrival will help you take care of these last-minute requests.

Get Acquainted

If you have not yet seen the deceased, go into the chapel or church building and stand a few moments by the casket. This will enable you to be past the initial shock. In addition, if you are not acquainted with the chapel it helps to know where you will stand and/or sit during the service. The more familiar you are with all the details the better. Some time ago at a service, I had finished the eulogy before I realized that there was no casket behind me as I had been talking. It was only a memorial service. If you are holding the service at the mortuary, the director will usually direct you to a clergyperson's study where you can wait and meditate until it is time for the service to begin. Someone will get you when it is time to start and usher you to your place.

I try to have firmly impressed on my mind the order of service, that is, when I will read, when I will pray, and when hymns will be sung or played. You can also, if you have not already done so, mark the Scriptures you will be using so you will have easy access to them, and read over your obituary notes carefully.

Make Copies

Have your secretary prepare copies of the order of service for you, the mortician, the soloist, the organist, and anyone else involved with the service. It will save time and embarrassing moments of uncertainty. Leave nothing to chance. If the funeral director is to close the service, it will help him or her to know how you will end the eulogy (directors do not always listen during the eulogy).

I also like to number the survivors on my notes so I will not miss them as I read the obituary, as in the following:

1. wife
2. first son
3. second son
4. first daughter
5. second daughter
6. fourteen grandchildren

Obviously, I don't read these aloud; the numbering helps me to keep in proper sequence so I don't forget anyone.

Overcome Your Jitters

After nearly three decades of conducting services, I still get nervous. But there are three basic and necessary ways to overcome nervousness as you wait for the service to begin. (1) Pray. Pray for God's wisdom, his strength, his consolation for the family. Pray often and pray boldly. (2) Prepare. You should always be prepared fully. If you are a novice you may wonder if there is such a thing as being fully prepared. The answer, of course, is relative, but you should by the time of the service have your eulogy fully written and you should have gone over it, rehearsing it several times so that you are comfortable with your notes. (3) Breathe out deeply several times. The idea is not to take deep breaths but to expel all the air from your lungs several times. This will have a calming effect on you.

Reassure the Family

Your confidence will help them and will help you, too. It will have the additional benefit of getting your mind off yourself.

If You Make a Mistake

If you commit a blunder, correct it quickly and go on. Not very long ago, during a funeral at our building, the order of service called for me to read a selection from Scripture and then to lead a prayer. I read the Scripture and had stepped off the raised platform before I remembered that I was to lead the prayer (I had not checked my own order of service). Trying to think quickly, I decided I should lead the prayer from where I was standing before all the mourners. I was able to do that all right, but I committed another blunder of an even worse kind. I said something like, "Lord, we are all here prostate before you." I quickly corrected it to *prostrate*. Amazingly, no one caught it or made an issue of it.

Speak to the Family Directly

While attending a funeral of a Jewish friend some years ago, my wife and I were impressed by the rabbi's delivery. One of his strengths was the firm eye contact that he continually made with the family and, to a lesser degree, with all of us. In any conversation it is important to make honest eye contact with your listeners. Be sure to talk with the family and mourners during your eulogy in this way.

Be Honest

A eulogy should not be a performance. It is not a place for theatrical or dramatic effects. You are there as a representative of the Lord and as a friend of the family. It is your purpose to help the mourners confront the reality of death, to come to terms with their loss, and to be confronted with God's love and his claim on our lives.

Stand by the Casket When You Are Finished

When you have concluded your part of the service, whether by prayer or not, walk to the casket and stand at the foot. If someone is assisting you in the service, he or she can stand at one end of the casket and you at the other.

This usually serves as a signal to the director that you have finished. The director at this point will come forward to direct the mourners so they can pass by the casket, view the remains to pay their respects, and then to go to the grave site. Remain by the casket until all the mourners have passed by.

Once the visitors are gone, the family is usually given an opportunity to see the deceased one more time. I have found it best to step back out of the way, but to watch for any family member who has a special need. This often will be the most emotional part of the service. If someone is especially hurting or grief stricken, you can put a hand on that person's shoulder to demonstrate your concern and support. Grievers should not feel rushed.

9

Important Miscellany

Charging for Your Services

In some religious persuasions it is customary to charge a fee for your services. After all, don't all other professional persons receive remuneration for their expertise? On the other hand, most ministers are paid by their churches. Should they charge church members for doing church work on church time?

I have had minister friends who do not accept any honorariums. I have heard of ministers and persons of the cloth who charge what I regard as exorbitant fees for their services.

My course has been never to charge a fee for a funeral. If you deal with a mortuary, it will usually be collected by them and then given to you by check on the day of the service. If the deceased was a member of your church, the mortuary will sometimes ask the family if they wish to pay you directly. Usually the funeral director will let you know of the family's decision. Frequently the family will offer you an envelope on the day of the service. At times they will pay you when you make your follow-up call on the home. When it is offered, I accept it with a warm thank you and state that it was not necessary. I have had a few families not offer anything—not even a thank you—but they have been very few.

In cases where the family was in hardship I have told them beforehand I wanted nothing and have returned it when they offered.

I have always believed that God will reward me if I do his will first and put money second. He is always faithful.

Making Follow-up Calls

When you leave the family on the day of the funeral, you can propose your calling on them in a few days. I try to make that call within three to seven days of the service. What is the purpose? To see how family members are doing. Sometimes they have a real letdown after all the out-of-town family members leave and after the initial rush of attention diminishes.

They should be encouraged to continue their quiet reflection. You can encourage church members to spend time with them. It is a great time for ministry. They are often more amenable to the word of God at this time in their lives than at any other.

But make sure they understand that your intentions are honorable, not amorous. If you are calling on a person of the opposite sex, take an older, sincere believer of the opposite sex with you so no misunderstandings can develop. Many years ago I believe I made a young woman uncomfortable by my offer to call on her later, even though I explained completely what my purpose was. And by calling on one older woman more than once, I created an extremely awkward situation for myself. She was forty years older than I and completely unattractive to me, but apparently because of her background she had only one interpretation of any interest shown in her. It's best to train church members to make follow-up calls on grievers and have them take over after the initial visit.

Dealing with Fraternal Orders

There are many persons in this country who belong to lodges and fraternal organizations. Most of these groups have a funeral ritual for their members. In some cases they will handle the whole service. In other cases the deceased or the deceased's family desires you to cooperate with the lodge members.

In conducting the service some ministers refuse to cooperate. You will have to decide on the basis of your conscience. It would help you to investigate the meaning of the service that they perform. In some instances the ritual has secret or hidden meaning that members must not reveal.

I have cooperated with fraternal orders, but I always insist that they complete their rituals before I begin. That way it is understood that what I say has no relationship with lodge ritual. Then I do my best to divorce the minds of the hearers from the previous ritual. This is the only way that I can conscientiously participate.

AIDS

In recent years AIDS, a problem unforeseen over the past centuries, has developed into a major concern. It has increasing complications and implications. Two questions are, what are the health risks of people at the service who may touch the deceased, and how should a minister direct his or her comments?

At the time of this writing the medical profession tells us that risk is only through transfer of blood or body fluids, so I don't feel there is great risk in the touch factor. Far more difficult for me has been what to say. I have done several services of persons who have died of AIDS. I frankly don't feel that a person who has contracted AIDS through homosexual activity is different in death from a miser, adulterer, gossip, or anyone whose life is not in order with God.

Only a person whose life is right with God has any hope, according to my convictions. We can never be sure where a person's heart is. In a few of those cases of AIDS victims there was sincere repentance before God. I believe if that repentance was sincere, God accepts them.

If you will note the sample eulogies I have included, I never say with confidence anyone is going to heaven or hell, because I don't know their hearts and minds. Only God knows that (see 1 Cor. 4:1–5). But I am convinced that one must be right with God to see him.

Dealing with Conflict

Occasionally family conflicts will erupt. Often you will become aware of them as you meet with the family to make arrangements. At times the grievers will speak of some estranged family member no one has seen; no one knows for sure whether he will appear or how he will behave. As the incidence of divorce increases there will be more situations of possible conflict among stepfamily members.

I have found it helpful to talk with the family beforehand as to possibility of conflict, if they bring up the subject, and review with them options for dealing with it. The options I suggest are along the lines of understanding and forgiveness.

Sometimes situations develop you are not prepared for. Many years ago at the close of a service, the wife and mother of the deceased argued over who would see him last before the casket was closed.

There are some rules of thumb I try to follow in these situations. First, I try to get all parties to work toward compromise.

Second, in the case of a minor, the parents' wishes should prevail. If it is a divided family, it should be the wishes of the parent who has custody of the child.

Third, the wishes that the deceased expressed in his or her will should be carried out.

Fourth, the wife's or husband's desire should be carried out before the parents', regardless of the age of the deceased.

Fifth, in the case of Christians, I try to get them to go the second mile in showing compassion and understanding in their relationships with non-Christians. I see this as a good opportunity for Christians to demonstrate God's love.

Sixth, if your conscience is compromised in any way, you can politely step out of it and courteously request that someone else not affected as you are conduct the service.

Seventh, in all cases I believe I must be true to the Word of God as I understand it. His will must prevail in all I do.

Open or Closed Caskets?

The "case is closed" by most people on the subject of viewing remains at services. Family members will often insist, "I want to remember Daddy as he was alive, not dead." The argument seems compelling and logical. If family members who are arranging the service are insistent enough, you will have no option. The casket will be closed. Others believe the casket should not be left open for other reasons. "Mom is not there," they may say. Or, it is "pagan to look at a corpse."

Probably the real issue for these people is that they are terrified of death. Over the years I've been interested in the body language of mourners who pass by the casket at the close of the service. Some will approach the casket directly, linger to sob, touch the corpse, and say their goodbyes. Others will make a sharp turn away from the casket as soon as they see the side exit. Fear of death at viewing time can almost be measured in feet and inches, or centimeters, if you will.

Some people have left prior instructions saying they want no viewing of their bodies when they are gone.

There are regional and cultural customs you need to investigate if you are a novice in the ministry or in your area of service.

In many cases, the family will ask your opinion regarding viewing. If you are either undecided or decided, you may want to consider another perspective on viewing remains. One of your purposes as a minister is to help people confront death. Viewing remains is a healthy step in the direction of confrontation. What the mourner must come to terms with is the finality of death. Seeing the loved one in the casket helps this to happen much sooner and more completely.

I believe it is very helpful for all concerned to have the casket open before or after the service. Whether it should be open during the service may be best decided by your own style of delivering eulogies. If you want people to hear your message in any context, you want as few distractions as possible—visual, audible, or otherwise. You will already be competing with flowers, latecomers, assorted sniffling and coughing (and even singing birds that some morticians enclose in their chapels). Fixing on the sight of an open casket may be an overpowering urge from which you will not be able to free some mourners.

On the other hand, I've seen some priests and ministers stand directly by an open casket and talk about the departed one very effectively. The choice here should be made according to your style.

10

Sample Eulogies

In some cases names and a few details in these sample eulogies are changed for the sake of privacy. I have followed the format outlined earlier in the book.

Sample Eulogy 1

This eulogy was given at the service of a man who died in middle age. His death was a result of the lifestyle he had followed most of his adult life. However, he made a serious commitment to God in his last days.

Text: Ephesians 2:4–9
Comments

It might seem contradictory to you to talk of God's love in the presence of death. His love seems remote. Suffering and death have prevailed again. It is true, as Shakespeare said, "We are cabined, cribbed, confined."

As was observed in the *Rubáiyát* of Omar Khayyám, "Strange—is it not?—that of the myriads who before us passed the door of darkness through, not one returns to tell us of the road, which we discover we must travel, too." We all lose this great conflict, this terrible struggle with death.

Death has many opening scenarios. A chest pain turning into a massive heart failure; the screeching and crashing of cars at an intersection; the sudden, violent quakes of the earth; the lost memory of Alzheimer's; the hard-fought battle against a raging disease—all of these are death's opening scenes. They are varied, but the stillness of death's final scene is always the same. Death always wins.

The great conflict of life and death transcends the human realm. That's one of the first things the Bible tells us.

God's creation is good and beautiful. But that goodness can be maintained only by serving and pleasing our Creator.

Our first ancestors believed the good was in possessions and enlightenment. They desired that fruit passionately. It deceived them as it deceives us. We spend our lives needing acceptance and love and understanding.

We allow ourselves to be deceived into thinking our possessions, power, and intelligence will fill that void within us. But they only make us more distant, alone, alienated.

As Caesar Borgia lamented, "I have provided in the course of my life for everything except death; and now, alas! I am to die entirely unprepared."

What can we do to prepare ourselves? How do we face this grisly foe? How do we deal with this awesome enemy? There are definite steps to victory.

First, we must admit, acknowledge—concede—how dreadfully death affects us, how mightily it controls us, how it haunts us in the night, stalks the recesses of our minds, assaults our tranquility.

Second, we must confess our own sin. John wrote in 1 John 1:9: "If we confess our sins, [God] is faithful and just and will forgive us our sins and purify us from all unrighteousness."

Third, when we lose a loved one, as we have today, we should spend time reflecting, remembering, reviewing.

John, Jewel, Ann, Marlene, there are, no doubt, vivid recollections of Bill's childhood or yours in Kansas. Perhaps it will center on Bill's love for classical music and the piano, his enormous compassion and kindness for you and his friends.

(Here a story about Bill's childhood given me by his sister was read.)

I first met Bill about thirty years ago and was always impressed by his gentlemanly, upbeat spirit, his sense of fairness and concern. Bill was gifted, artistic, was a successful wigmaker and stylist. He made the elderly look younger and helped those undergoing chemotherapy to restore their dignity.

In the world, among people, Bill was successful and was loved by nearly everyone. But many of the things we tend to value in varying degrees were extremely important to him.

He loved silver; was possessed by it.

He was always meticulous about his appearance.

He also followed a lifestyle advocated by the world.

He allowed himself to be deceived by lust of the eyes, lust of flesh, and pride of life.

As our text in Ephesians said, "All of us also lived among them at one time, gratifying the cravings of our sinful nature and following its desires and thoughts." He was "dead in transgressions."

As Ann mentioned, "Bill grew up in a home where he heard about Jesus but never really came to know him, that is, until the last three months of his life." Then he fell in love with God. Bill came to understand the deceitfulness of possessions and position. Ann noted, "His desire for material possessions peeled off like layers of old paint."

That meticulous desire for an unblemished physical appearance was discarded. Though he knew his condition was likely terminal, he wanted you his friends and others to know about Jesus, to turn from vanity and carnal ways.

When Bill first learned of his condition he responded by saying, "I'm not afraid. If this is what it takes for God to get my attention, I'm glad." He firmly believed these statements from Scripture:

If anyone is in Christ, he is a new creation; the old has gone (2 Cor. 5:17).

But because of his great love for us, God, who is rich in mercy, made us alive with Christ even when we were dead in transgressions—it is by grace you have been saved. And God raised us up with Christ and seated us with him in the heavenly realms in Christ Jesus, in order that in the coming ages he might show the incomparable riches of his grace, expressed in his kindness to us in Christ Jesus. For it is by grace you have been saved, through faith—and this not . . . by works, so that no one can boast (Eph. 2:4–9).

Bill came to understand God's grace in many ways. First, he knew that we are saved by grace, not by works. Romans 8:1 says: "Therefore, there is now no condemnation for those who are in Christ Jesus." What a wonderful feeling to know that God has saved us by his mercy; it is not earned or purchased or bought. It is paid for fully by the sacrifice of Jesus.

Second, as the writer of Hebrews declared, God has said: "Never will I leave you; never will I forsake you" (Heb. 13:5). Bill's physical condition required almost constant attention over the past several weeks, and the Lord provided a team. It consisted of Larry, his long-time friend, whom God helped overcome disease in his life so that he could be available; Ann, who was able to help over the summertime and utilized vacation time; Constance, who had been hospitalized because of severe struggles, but functioned beautifully to assist. All three felt privileged to serve him. His dear friend, Francine, called daily with words of encouragement and love.

God did not forsake Bill. In fact, Bill rejoiced in Christ each day. The words of Paul to the Philippians encouraged him:

Do not be anxious about anything, but in everything, by prayer and petition, with thanksgiving, present your requests to God. And the peace of God, which transcends all understanding, will guard your hearts and your minds in Christ Jesus (Phil. 4:6, 7).

Jesus urged his disciples not to fret or be fearful: "Do not let your hearts be troubled. Trust in God; trust also in me. In my father's house are many rooms" (John 14:1).

How could Jesus say this? (1) He is God's one and only son. He lived a perfect life and was tempted in every way, as we are, yet without sinning. (2) He was everything the prophets said in Scriptures he should be: born in Bethlehem, reared in Nazareth, and pierced for our transgressions. (3) He was crucified for our failure. (4) God raised him on the third day. According to 1 Corinthians 15 he was seen by more than five hundred witnesses at one time. (5) Jesus is now at God's right hand.

God gives us this promise: If we will turn away from our vain quests and empty pursuits, our pride, and turn to him—to belief in his son, Jesus—God grants us victory over death.

Listen, I tell you a mystery: We will not all sleep, but we will all be changed—in a flash, in the twinkling of an eye, at the last trumpet. For the trumpet will sound, the dead will be raised imperishable, and we will be changed. For the perishable must clothe itself with the imperishable, and the mortal with immortality. When the perishable has been clothed with the imperishable, and the mortal with immortality, then the saying that is written will come true: "Death has been swallowed up in victory" (1 Cor. 15:51–54).

The promise of resurrection, I know, sounds unbelievable to modern minds. It was just as incredible to ancient people. In response, I'd like to tell a story I read some years ago.

Many years ago a boy spent the day fishing on the banks of the Mississippi. The fishing was not good that day, but there was an old man fishing nearby, and the two began to chat. Their conversation went on amiably until dusk, when a stern-wheeler could be seen off in the distance plying up the river. As soon as the boy saw the river boat, he began to jump up and down. Pulling his red handkerchief from his hip pocket, he waved it, hoping to catch the attention of someone on the boat. Observing the boy's behavior, the old man chided his younger companion, "Son, what you are doing is stupid. No boat like that is going to stop for a little boy." The old man went back to his fishing. He looked up later to see that the boat was actually slowing down and approaching the bank where they were standing. A gangplank was lowered, and the little boy excitedly jumped on board to hugs from the crew. But he turned back to the old man, remonstrating, "I'm not stupid, Mister. My daddy is the captain of this river boat, and we're on our way to a new home upriver."

In the same way, we believe that Jesus is the captain of our salvation and will gladly come back for us to take us to our new home in heaven.

Sample Eulogy 2

This eulogy was given at the grave side of a boy about two years old. He died after prolonged suffering from congenital problems.

Text: Matthew 19:13, 14
Comments

We have come to share with Charles and Linda and their families in the loss of Eric. We have come to weep with them, to feel with them the keen sense of separation, to wonder in anguish, to ask for understanding and forgiveness from our mutual father, God, to share in a profoundly painful and vexing moment.

We do not come today with any glib answers. Our hearts are shattered as we stand here in grief. To see life cut so extremely short is stressful and difficult to understand. We can't help thinking what might have been. At this, anger and frustration well up within us.

Though I believe that God would prefer that we honestly express our anguish, verbalize our fears, and speak of the hopes now dashed, there is one thing we must not do. We cannot let our guilt overwhelm us or divide us in our love for one another. We need to openly express our feelings of guilt for our past behaviors so God's healing can take place. As the apostle John instructed, "If we confess our sins, [God] is faithful and just and will forgive us our sins and purify us from all unrighteousness" (1 John 1:9). We want Charles and Linda to know of our love and support for them.

One thing we all must do is positively affirm the constant care of God. Jesus personified that love as he blessed and prayed for the children brought to him. It is instructive that Jesus' concern and love for little children rose up in spite of the mire of selfishness and calloused ambition of adults.

God also proved, beyond all human questionings and doubts, his love for us through his own suffering and anguish. He stood by and watched as his only son's life was taken from him. Though God could have acted to save Jesus, he did not do so, to show that even at the pinnacle of man's wickedness God's love and forgiving nature could be displayed for all time. We have the assurance of God's care. As Jesus declared, "I give them eternal life and they shall never perish, and no one shall snatch them out of my hand."

I am confident that Charles and Linda feel that expectancy of David. When the infant son born of Bathsheba died, David was well aware of the fixed manner of life and death, as seen in his question: "Can I bring him back again?" Though David knew that was impossible, he did express a great hope and expectancy: "I will go to him, but he will not return to me" (2 Sam. 12:23). We believe that Eric is safe in the hands of God, and that Charles and Linda, and all of us, can go to be with him.

The Book of Revelation describes that hope for which we long:

> Then I saw a new heaven and a new earth, for the first heaven and the first earth had passed away, and there was no longer any sea. I saw the Holy City, the new Jerusalem, coming down out of heaven from God, prepared as a bride beautifully dressed for her husband. And I heard a loud voice from the throne saying, "Now the dwelling of God is with men, and he will live with them. They will be his people, and God himself will be with them and be their God. He will wipe away every tear from their eyes. There will be no more death or mourning or crying or pain, for the old order of things has passed away" (Rev. 21:1–4).

Sample Eulogy 3

This service was prepared for a woman in her late seventies who died as she was preparing to move out of state to live with her daughter. She had been a church member for about five years.

Text: Romans 8:38, 39
Comments

This is one of the most sublime and assuring promises ever made. The source of it is God himself who promises that no power can separate one of his children from him. No power on earth or heaven, no power of the present or the future can affect the one trusting in Jesus.

It is not by accident that Paul mentioned death first in the order of all the threats that interfere with our relationship with God. It is in the presence of death that we feel most alone, most threatened, most fearful and anxious. Death strikes us all. It usually leaves the survivors pervaded with guilt and terror. The prophet Isaiah aptly described death as "the covering that is cast over all peoples, the veil that is spread over all nations . . . the reproach of his people" (Isa. 25:7, 8 RSV).

Paul defined it as the last enemy to be destroyed. Because death is inextricably bound up with our sin and is the wages of sin, it is awesome and fearsome. It is unremitting. We come today to admit its power and the hold it has over all flesh.

We feel the stark contrast between a few days ago when Emma was so vibrant, so alive, so filled with expectancy, and the present silence and solicitude. Our remembrances of Emma are images of her energetic approach to life. There was no blandness in her. She dressed colorfully, expressed herself vividly, and was always vivacious.

Emma was a trained dietician. She majored in home economics at the university and always had a creative interest in food and nutrition. Her neighbors shared in the tastes and aromas of her homemade pies and cakes.

Emma had an active, indomitable spirit. She worked hard to help Susan get through college. She was employed by (company name) and later by (company name), where she was a valuable part of the corporation. She applied the same sense of industry and organization during her preparations to move in the past few months. A caring, giving person, she loved people. By the testimony of her family she was also "a great baby-sitter."

Susan and her family were the great love of Emma's life. She spoke often of them and always proudly. Susan is thankful for the strong, loving relationship her mother and she had from earliest times. Emma held her son-in-law in greatest esteem and spoke proudly of her grandchildren. What vivid recollections we all shall always possess of the broad, warm smile and the brightness of her eyes! We treasure them.

Emma was not perfect. Our grief has not occluded her foibles, nor do we desire that. She could speak with a resolute directness that caused you to cower. But it is the faults and weaknesses she had and that we all possess, most of us to a greater degree than Emma, that make us understand that we all need help.

We were all placed on this earth by our Creator to praise him, to love and honor all of his other creatures and creation. We have failed miserably in God's intention for us. He is holy and good. In contrast, we often choose lifestyles, thought patterns, and ambitions that separate us from God. We are involved with sin and death. That's why Jesus came from God: to show us the beauty of a lifestyle of love—a love so true and firmly fixed that he voluntarily died to pay the penalty of our failure.

Then came the most marvelous miracle of history: he was alive again three days later. It is a fact witnessed by five hundred persons at one time. Where is Jesus now? At the right hand of God pleading, interceding with the Father for those who trust and believe him. The writer of Hebrews made reference to what we have just related: first, our responsibility to God; second, our need of the help offered in his son; third, the willingness and the ability he has to help us. The New

Testament assures us: "Nothing in all creation is hidden from God's sight. Everything is uncovered and laid bare before the eyes of him to whom we must give account" (Heb. 4:13).

> Therefore, since we have a great high priest who has gone through the heavens, Jesus the Son of God, let us hold firmly to the faith we profess. For we do not have a high priest who is unable to sympathize with our weaknesses, but we have one who has been tempted in every way, just as we are, yet was without sin. Let us then approach the throne of grace with confidence, so that we may receive mercy and find grace to help us in our time of need (see Heb. 4:13–16).

I said earlier that the two things most common in the presence of death are guilt and terror. We don't have to approach this day with dread and apprehension. Praise God that both guilt and terror are removed by the presence of Jesus who holds us permanently in the Father.

Because he died to pay the penalty of our guilt, forgiveness is available to those who will claim it. The apostle John promised: "If we confess our sins, God is faithful and just and will forgive us our sins and purify us from all unrighteousness" (1 John 1:9).

Though fear of death keeps many of us in bondage, even death's terror has been removed. Jesus destroyed him who has the power over death. We can join him in his resurrection. Thank God, Emma shared that hope. She came to know her Lord and Creator in recent years, studied with many of us on Thursdays, and was maturing in him.

What a difference it makes when we are prepared for this day in Christ because we know that "neither death nor life, neither angels nor demons, neither the present nor the future, nor any powers, neither height nor depth, nor anything else in all creation, will be able to separate us from the love of God that is in Christ Jesus our Lord" (Rom. 8:38–39).

We shall close with the great resurrection assurance Paul wrote to those grieving Greeks centuries ago:

Brothers, we do not want you to be ignorant about those who fall asleep, or to grieve like the rest of men, who have no hope. We believe that Jesus died and rose again and so we believe that God will bring with Jesus those who have fallen asleep in him. According to the Lord's own word, we tell you that we who are still alive, who are left till the coming of the Lord, will certainly not precede those who have fallen asleep. For the Lord himself will come down from heaven, with a loud command, with the voice of the archangel and with the trumpet call of God, and the dead in Christ will rise first. After that, we who are still alive and are left will be caught up with them in the clouds to meet the Lord in the air. And so we will be with the Lord forever. Therefore encourage each other with these words (1 Thess. 4:13–18).

Sample Eulogy 4

This eulogy was delivered at the service for a woman in her eighties who had been a long-time member of the church and had taught Sunday school for many years.

Text: 1 Thessalonians 4:13–18
Comments

We are gathered to pay our respects to Esta, to grieve for her, but to also exult in the victory of our Savior.

(Following the obituary, stating birth, marriage, and survivors, I continued.) She had been a teacher in Northern California and Nevada and then taught for several years at Pacific Christian Academy in Graton, California.

She and her husband, along with her brother and his wife, were instrumental in starting the Church of Christ in Sebastopol, California, about 1948. They constructed the building literally by hand. We want to review Esta's life more at length.

Esta's long-time friend, whose three children were all taught by her, will lead us in two hymns: "Safe in the Arms of Jesus," and "The New Song." Following that, our associate minister will read Psalm 23. An elder of the church, whose four children were all taught by Esta, will direct us in prayer.

(Following this, I began the eulogy.)

"His loved ones are very precious to him and he does not lightly let them die" (Ps. 116:15 LB).

Esta had marked this verse in her Living Bible, the verse that is rendered by many translations: "Precious in the sight of the LORD is the death of his saints."

The awareness of our finitude, of the brevity and frailty of our lives haunts us. Every generation since Adam has been anxious. We are, "through fear of death, subject to life-long bondage." Life is tenuous, fragile. It is unpredictable. It often takes sudden turns that find us unprepared.

To unbelievers there seems a randomness about life wherein there is fortune or misfortune depending on nothing more meaningful than the flip of a coin or the throw of the dice. There are those who have good runs of chance, but at some point one's luck must run out.

Even believers, those whose faith is strong, look askance at the events of life. They are aware of God's presence and power. They know his creative activity. For them the crucial question is: Does God care about what happens to us? Does he forget our personal needs, our fears, our wants, our need for his presence?

Thus David himself began Psalm 13 wrestling with those vexing questions that wrench and strain the minds of believers: "How long, O LORD? Will you forget me forever? How long will you hide your face from me? How long must I wrestle with my thoughts and every day have sorrow in my heart? . . . Look on me and answer, O LORD my God."

The difficulty we have understanding God's ways can be stated no more forthrightly than by a young lad who reasoned, "I don't think God is fair. He lets us die. But he doesn't die himself."

It is because this young man's two main premises were misguided that he came to the wrong conclusion about God's fairness. God does not desire our death. Neither does he sit by idly while we die.

Esta knew well the truth of that. That's why the passage, "His loved ones are very precious to him and he does not lightly let them die" was marked in her Bible.

Helen Keller once noted: "Unless we form the habit of going to the Bible in bright moments as well as in trouble, we cannot fully respond to its consolations because we lack equilibrium between light and darkness."

Few people have ever achieved that balance of Bible knowledge, but Esta did.

Esta had numerous talents; her creativity expressed itself in many ways. She loved to write, to paint, to sew. She made many of her daughter's clothes. She loved to entertain, to cook. She was famous for her homemade bread and boysenberry cobbler. As her brother, George, commented, "There were not enough hours for her in a day."

Her greatest desire for others was for them to see what God has done for the world in Christ. She had a special gift for enabling and motivating young people to comprehend the truth of Scripture.

She heartily agreed with Samuel Chadwick's observation that "no man is uneducated who knows the Bible, and no one is wise who is ignorant of its teachings."

One of the most significant things she did was to put together a book on Christ in the Old Testament, researching and assembling information given her by her uncle. It is a marvelous review of symbols and prophecies of Christ found throughout the Old Testament prophets.

It was at Esta's behest that I began writing lessons on the Old Testament predictions of the Messiah and their fulfillment. It has launched me on a lifelong project.

She deeply respected God's Word. She instilled that respect in her students. To Esta the promises of God were vibrantly alive. Those who studied under her were impressed by God's influence and power.

The gift of teaching did not come easily to Esta. She gave arduous hours to study and to perfecting her teaching skills. She committed much Scripture to memory and demanded that her students do the same. She gave them lessons that required considerable homework and preparation. They were not disdainful or scornful of her demands. Instead, they esteemed her and came to reverence the Word.

My wife and I are thankful that all of our children were able to study under her. Every parent I have ever known here has shared that same joy. She continued to teach and inspire until well into her eighty-first year.

In her final illness she received many calls and notes from former students.One young man wrote:

> Dear Esta:
>
> How I love you for teaching me about God; for fueling the spark that lit this soul on fire; for making classes fun and learning simple.
>
> But most of all I love you for showing me our Father's love through your life and actions. Things that cannot be taught in class—the never-ending lesson of life and love—you have shown to me and is forever living in my soul.
>
> Love that endures forever,
> Steve

One young woman wrote:

> Dear Esta:
>
> I just wanted to tell you I've been thinking of you and hope you feel a lot better. I hope to see you soon. If I don't come in time, I'll surely see you in heaven!
>
> I love you lots!!
> Love, Kari
>
> P.S. Thank you for teaching me to be a Christian. I'm holding you up in my prayers.

Esta's own daughter and son know well the beauty of their mother's devotion to them, the strength of her faith.

Esta was not perfect. The only perfection she would ever have claimed is the perfection of God's love in Christ.

But there was an unwavering hope in her that "God's loved ones are very precious to him and he does not lightly let them die."

The confidence she had in our Lord was resolute even to her death.

Rare is that one who along with Paul would say, "For me to live is Christ, and to die is gain. That with full courage

now as always Christ will be honored in my body, whether by
life or by death" (Phil. 1:21, 20 RSV).

During many recent Sundays large groups would gather
around Esta's bed to sing hymns of faith, read Scripture, to
pray, and share communion with her. She knew she was in
her last days. But as the Scriptures were read and as hymns
were sung, she had what can be described best as a beatific
visage, "as though it were the face of an angel."

Her trust has made a lasting impact. One long-time friend
wrote Esta's daughter: "May you find comfort in knowing
what a beautiful legacy your mother left. She touched my
life, as one of many, and made me a better person. She will
live in my heart always."

Esta would insist, of course, that it is all from the Lord
who made heaven and earth. The passage she asked to be
read most often in her final days was Romans 8. Some
selected verses from the great chapter (Rom. 8:28–39) affirm
the joy and beauty of life trusting in Christ.

What was the foundation of Esta's hope? It is that God
does not take lightly either our sin or our death. She was
awed by the implications of 2 Corinthians 5:21: "God made
him who had no sin to be sin for us, so that in him we might
become the righteousness of God."

Jesus died to put away our sin from us. We are precious to
him. And he was raised to show that God does not take our
death lightly, either.

So will it be with the resurrection of the dead. The body that
is sown is perishable, it is raised imperishable; it is sown in
dishonor, it is raised in glory; it is sown in weakness, it is
raised in power; it is sown a natural body, it is raised a spiritual body (1 Cor. 15:42–44).

Listen, I tell you a mystery: We will not all sleep, but we will
all be changed—in a flash, in the twinkling of an eye, at the
last trumpet. For the trumpet will sound, the dead will be
raised imperishable, and we will be changed. For the perishable must clothe itself with the imperishable, and the mortal

with immortality. When the perishable has been clothed with the imperishable, and the mortal with immortality, then the saying that is written will come true: "Death has been swallowed up in victory" (1 Cor. 15:51–54).

Therefore, my dear brothers, stand firm. Let nothing move you. Always give yourselves fully to the work of the Lord, because you know that your labor in the Lord is not in vain (1 Cor. 15:58).

Resources for Funeral Messages

How to Use This Section

In Part 2 of the book you will find Scriptures, poems, hymns, and a sample committal prayer.

The Scriptures are indexed by subject. An index of poems by subject is followed by the poems alphabetical by title. Some of the poems are too long to read in their entirety. They are included because you may find some lines to fit your particular situation. For example, see "On an Infant Dying as Soon as Born," pp. 110, 111, lines 29 and 30: "The stern-eyed fate descry, that babe or mother, one must die." You may have to give a eulogy for an infant whose death was due to the above circumstance. It is probably unwise to attempt reading more than eight to ten lines at once.

Hymns are listed alphabetically, preceded by suggestions for use.

Following a sample committal prayer are a few poems based on Scripture to accompany your prayer and Scripture reading at grave side or niche side.

11

Scriptures by Subject

When whole chapters are listed, I'm indicating that most of the verses in the chapter are helpful. However, it is probably wise to use selected verses and to avoid lengthy readings.

Adversity, patience in	James 5:7–11
Age and youth	Ecclesiastes 12:1
Appeal for God to hear	Psalm 119:169
Appeal for God's care	Psalm 17:6–8
Appeal for God's mercy	Jeremiah 10:23, 24
	Habakkuk 3:2
Appeal for mercy	Psalm 6
Appeal for relief	Psalm 4
Appeal to God for help	Psalm 121
Atoning sacrifice of Jesus	1 John 2:12

Believers, confidence of	1 John 5:13–15
Benediction	1 Peter 5:10, 11
	Hebrews 13:20, 21
	Jude 24, 25
Blessed are the dead in Christ	Revelation 14:13
Blessing	Numbers 6:24–26
	2 Corinthians 13:14

Book of life	Daniel 12:1–3
	Revelation 20:11–15
Brevity of life	Psalm 39:1–7
	James 4:13–17
Brevity and uncertainty of life	Job 16:18–22
	Job 17:1, 11

Children, God's care for	Matthew 18:1–3
	Matthew 18:10–14
	Mark 10:13–16
Christ, hope in	1 Thessalonians 4:13–18
Christ's saving work	Hebrews 2:5–18
Comfort for the weary	Isaiah 40:28–31
Comfort in suffering	2 Corinthians 1:3, 4
Confidence in God's care	Psalm 23:6
Confidence in obedience	1 John 3:21–24
Confidence of believers	1 John 5:13–15
Confidence of faithful life	2 Timothy 4:1–8
Consolation	Matthew 11:28–30

Day of the Lord described	2 Peter 3:10–13
Dead in Christ blessed	Revelation 14:13
Death defeated	Isaiah 25:6–9
Death of infant	Isaiah 65:20
Death, man forsaken	Psalm 22:15
Death, no ransom for	Psalm 49:7–9
	Psalm 49:12–14
Death, preparing for	1 Peter 4:7–11
Death, need to prepare for	Luke 12:16–21
Death and judgment, need to prepare for	1 Thessalonians 5:4–11
	Titus 2:11–14
	Hebrews 3:12–15
Death's threat	Psalm 18:1–6
Distress	Psalm 102:23–28
	Psalm 4

Earthquake, death from	Psalm 60:1–5
Eternal life, certainty of	2 Samuel 12:13–23
Eternal nature of God	Hebrews 1:10–12
Expressions of desolation	Psalm 77:1–12

God's wisdom	Romans 11:33–36
Good life rewarded	Matthew 25:31–46
Greatness and sovereignty of God	Psalm 8
Guilt, help with	Psalm 32:1–7

Healing after tragedy	Hosea 6:1–3
Heaven as goal	Philippians 3:12–14
	Philippians 3:20–21
	Colossians 3:1–4
Heaven described	Isaiah 65:17–25
	Revelation 21:1–5
	Revelation 21:10–27
Heaven's glory described	Revelation 7:9–17
Heaven's praise and rejoicing	Revelation 19:4–10
Help in dealing with guilt	Psalm 32:1–7
Hiddenness of God	Psalm 102:1–3
	Habakkuk 1:2–4
Hope in Christ	1 Thessalonians 4:13–18
Hope in righteousness	Psalm 37:18
Hope in suffering	Romans 5:1–5

Infant death	Isaiah 65:20

Jesus, atoning sacrifice of	1 John 2:1, 2
Jesus, first and last	Revelation 22:13
Judgment (also see Death and judgment)	Revelation 22:12
Judgment, certainty of	Hebrews 9:26b–28
Justice of God	Psalm 11

Keys of death, Christ holding	Revelation 1:12–18

Lack of faith	Luke 8:22–25
Love defined	1 Corinthians 13:1–13
Love of God	Psalm 63:1–8
	Romans 8:31–39
Life, book of	Daniel 12:1–3
Life, brevity of	Psalm 39:1–7
	James 4:13–17
Life, brevity and uncertainty	Job 17:1–11
Life, of few days and full of trouble	Job 14:1–14

Life, tree of	Revelation 22:14
Life, tree of and river of	Revelation 22:1-5

Man forsaken in death	Psalm 22:1-5
Man's helplessness before God[1]	Job 4:7-21
Man's helplessness in death	Job 1:21
Men born to trouble[1]	Job 5:7-11
Men like grass	1 Peter 1:22-25
Mercy, appeal for	Psalm 6
Mercy of God	Jonah 2:1-9
Mercy, plea for	Psalm 51:1-12
Mother and wife	Proverbs 31:10-31
Mourning	Acts 9:32-42

Nearness of God	Psalm 145:18

Obedience, confidence in	1 John 3:21-24
Old age described metaphorically	Ecclesiastes 12

Patience in adversity	James 5:7-11
Plea for mercy	Psalm 51:1-12
Plea of a dying man	Psalm 88
Praise God for greatness	Psalm 103:1-5
	Psalm 103:8-22
Preparing for death and judgment	1 Thessalonians 5:4-11
	Titus 2:11-14
	Hebrews 3:12-15
Preparing for death, need for	Luke 12:16-21
Promise of Christ to one who overcomes	Revelation 2:7
	Revelation 2:11
	Revelation 2:17
	Revelation 2:26-29
	Revelation 3:5
	Revelation 3:12
	Revelation 3:21

Raising of young man (Eutychus)	Acts 20:7-12

1. Though there are some good observations in these texts and they are often used in funerals, as you will notice, they are the words of Eliphaz the Temanite. God was not too pleased with his advice. Use it carefully.

Renewal through God's compassion	Lamentations 3:17–33
Resurrection	Ezekiel 37:5
	Daniel 12:2
	Hosea 13:14
	Psalm 49:15
Resurrection and gospel	1 Corinthians 15:1–11
Resurrection, certainty	1 Corinthians 15:12–28
Resurrection, confidence in	Job 19:25–27
Resurrection, description	1 Corinthians 15:35–58
	1 John 3:1–3
Resurrection, home with God	2 Corinthians 5:1–10
Resurrection, hope for	Philippians 3:7–11
Resurrection, judgment	John 5:19–30
Resurrection of Lazarus	John 11:1–44
Resurrection, living hope	1 Peter 1:3–9
Resurrection of believers	John 6:40
	2 Corinthians 4:7–18
Resurrection of Jesus	Matthew 28:1–10
	John 20:1–8
	John 20:10–18
	John 20:24–31
Resurrection, redemption of bodies	Romans 8:18–27
Resurrection, young man	Luke 7:11–16
Reward for fearing God	Psalm 60:1–4
Reward for good life	Matthew 25:31–46
Righteousness, hope in	Psalm 37:18
River of life	Revelation 22:1–5

Salvation	Psalm 73:21–28
Salvation in God	Psalm 62:1, 2
	Psalm 62:5–8
Saving work of Christ	Hebrews 2:5–18
Seasons and times	Ecclesiastes 3:1, 2
Strength from God	Isaiah 41:10
Suffering, comfort in	2 Corinthians 1:3, 4
Suffering, hope in	Romans 5:1–5
Sympathy of God	Hebrews 4:14–16

Times and seasons for everything	Ecclesiastes 3
Tree of life	Revelation 22:14
Tree of life, river of life	Revelation 22:1–5

Vision of Christ, holding keys of death   Revelation 1:12–18

Wailing and anguish in streets   Amos 5:16, 17
Waiting on God   Psalm 130:5
Weary, comfort for   Isaiah 40:28–31
Wife and mother   Proverbs 31:10–31
Wisdom of God   Romans 11:33–36

Young man, godly   Proverbs 4:1–12
Youth and age   Ecclesiastes 12:1

12

Poems

Index of Topics

Courage facing death
  Prospice   Robert Browning

Death, conflict over
  The Dead   Rupert Brooke

Death, finality of
  Break, Break, Break   Alfred, Lord Tennyson

Death of a leader
  O Captain! My Captain!   Walt Whitman

Death, preparedness for
  Finis   Walter Savage Landor

Death, stillness of
  The Harp That Once Through Tara's Halls   Thomas Moore

Death, victory over
  Death   John Donne

Death where body has perished
or is in unknown location
  Monica's Last Prayer   Matthew Arnold

Faith in God's promises
  God Is   Pearl Pierson

Friend, loss of
  First Line: *When to the Sessions
  of Sweet Silent Thought*   William Shakespeare

God, confidence in
  Fortress of Hope   Anonymous

God as refuge
  Psalm 91   Thomas Carew

Good life characterized
  Character of a Happy Life   Sir Henry Wotton

Heaven
    Vital Spark of the Heavenly Flame   Alexander Pope

Hope in Christ
    Crossing the Bar   Alfred, Lord Tennyson
    Forever the Accepted Time   Pearl Pierson
    I Know That My Redeemer Lives   Charles Wesley
    When We Suffer Grief and Anguish   Pearl Pierson
    A Widow Grieving For Her Son   Pearl Pierson

Infant, death of
    On an Infant Dying as Soon as Born   Charles Lamb

Loneliness
    Monody   Herman Melville
    Go from Me   Elizabeth Barret Browning

Life, brevity of
    On Time   John Milton
    Revolutions   William Shakespeare
    River of Life   Thomas Campbell
    Rubáiyát of Omar Khayyám LXIII   Edward Fitzgerald
    Youth and Age   Samuel Taylor Coleridge

Life, purpose of
    Oh, Yet We Trust   Alfred, Lord Tennyson

Life, seasons of
    The Human Seasons   John Keats

Life, uncertainty of
    Dover Beach   Matthew Arnold

Man of strong character
    Herrick's Cavalier   Robert Herrick

Meaning of life
    Tempt Me No More   C. Day Lewis

Military person
    Soldier, Rest   Sir Walter Scott

Mystery of death
  Rubáiyát of Omar Khayyám LXIV   Edward Fitzgerald

Mystery of life
  Life, I Know Not What Thou Art   Anna Letitia Barbauld

Pain in saying goodbye
  The Journey Onwards   Thomas Moore

Peaceful death of a woman
  The Death Bed   Thomas Hood

Peace
  He Does Not Fear the Raging Sea   Pearl Pierson

Resurrection
  In Cycle Growth, Life Moves Along   Pearl Pierson
  The Evening Watch   Henry Vaughan

Suicide
  Richard Cory   Edwin Arlington Robinson

Uncertainty of life
  When I Have Fears   John Keats

Untimely death of a humble man
  The Man Named Legion   Sara Henderson Hay

Wife, loss of
  On His Deceased Wife   John Milton

Woman, death of
  Requiescat   Matthew Arnold

The following poems are alphabetical by title.

An Irish Airman Foresees His Death

I know that I shall meet my fate
Somewhere among the clouds above;
Those that I fight I do not hate,
Those that I guard I do not love;
My country is Kiltartan Cross,
My countrymen Kiltartan's poor,
No likely end could bring them loss
Or leave them happier than before.
Nor law, nor duty bade me fight,
Nor public men, nor cheering crowds,
A lonely impulse of delight
Drove to this tumult in the clouds;
I balanced all, brought all to mind,
The years to come seemed waste of breath,
A waste of breath the years behind
In balance with this life, this death.
—William Butler Yeats

Character of a Happy Life

How happy is he born and taught
That serveth not another's will;
Whose armour is his honest thought,
And simple truth his utmost skill!

Whose passions not his masters are,
Whose soul is still prepared for death;
Untied unto the world by care
Of public fame, or private breath;

Who envies none that chance doth raise,
Nor vice; who never understood
How deepest wounds are given by praise;
Nor rules of state, but rules of good;

Who hath his life from rumors freed,
Whose conscience is his strong retreat;
Whose state can neither flatterers feed,
Nor ruin make oppressors great;

Who God doth late and early pray
More of His grace than gifts to lend;
And entertains the harmless day
With a religious book or friend;

This man is freed from servile bands
Of hope to rise, or fear to fall;
Lord of himself, though not of lands;
And having nothing, yet hath all.
                          —Sir Henry Wotton

Crossing the Bar

Sunset and evening star,
    And one clear call for me!
And may there be no moaning of the bar,
    When I put out to sea,

But such a tide as moving seems asleep,
    Too full for sound and foam,
When that which drew from out the boundless deep
    Turns again home.

Twilight and evening bell,
    And after that the dark!
And may there be no sadness of farewell,
    When I embark;

For tho' from out our bourne of Time and Place
    The flood may bear me far,
I hope to see my Pilot face to face
    When I have crossed the bar.
                          —Alfred, Lord Tennyson

The Dead

These hearts were woven of human joys and cares,
    Washed marvellously with sorrow, swift to mirth.
The years had given them kindness. Dawn was theirs,
    And sunset, and the colors of the earth.
These had seen movement, and heard music; known
    Slumber and waking; loved; gone proudly friended;

Felt the quick stir of wonder; sat alone;
　　Touched flowers and furs and cheeks. All this is ended.
There are waters blown by changing winds to laughter
And lit by the rich skies, all day. And after,
　　Frost, with a gesture, stays the waves that dance
And wandering loveliness. He leaves a white
　　Unbroken glory, a gathered radiance,
A width, a shining peace, under the night.

　　　　　　　　　　　　　　　　　—Rupert Brooke

The Death Bed

We watch'd her breathing thro' the night,
　　Her breathing soft and low,
As in her breast the wave of life
　　Kept heaving to and fro.

But when the morn came dim and sad
　　And chill with early showers,
Her quiet eyelids closed—she had
　　Another morn than ours.

　　　　　　　　　　　　　　　　　—Thomas Hood

Death

Death be not proud, though some have callèd thee
Mighty and dreadful, for, thou art not so;
For, those whom thou think'st thou dost overthrow
Die not, poor death; nor yet canst thou kill me.
From rest and sleep, which but thy pictures be,
Much pleasure; then from thee, much more must flow;
And soonest our best men with thee do go,
Rest of their bones, and souls' delivery.
Thou art slave to fate, chance, kings, and desperate men,
And dost with poison, war, and sickness dwell,
And poppy, or charms can make us sleep as well,
And better than thy stroke; Why swell'st thou then?
One short sleep past, we wake eternally,
And death shall be no more; death, thou shalt die.

　　　　　　　　　　　　　　　　　—John Donne

Dover Beach

The sea is calm tonight.
The tide is full, the moon lies fair
Upon the straits; on the French coast the light
Gleams and is gone; the cliffs of England stand
Glimmering and vast, out in the tranquil bay.

Come to the window, sweet is the night air!
Only, from the long line of spray
Where the sea meets the moon-blanched land,
Listen! you hear the grating roar
Of pebbles which the waves draw back, and fling,
At their return, up the high strand,
Begin, and cease, and then again begin,
With tremulous cadence slow, and bring
The eternal note of sadness in.

Sophocles long ago
Heard it on the Ægean, and it brought
Into his mind the turbid ebb and flow
Of human misery; we
Find also in the sound a thought,
Hearing it by this distant northern sea.

The Sea of Faith
Was once, too, at the full, and round earth's shore
Lay like the folds of a bright girdle furled.
But now I only hear
Its melancholy, long, withdrawing roar,
Retreating, to the breath
Of the night wind, down the vast edges drear
And naked shingles of the world.

Ah, love, let us be true
To one another! for the world, which seems
To lie before us like a land of dreams,
So various, so beautiful, so new,
Hath really neither joy, nor love, nor light,
Nor certitude, nor peace, nor help for pain;
And we are here as on a darkling plain

Swept with confused alarms of struggle and flight,
Where ignorant armies clash by night.
                                          —Matthew Arnold

Finis

I strove with none, for none was worth my strife.
Nature I loved and, next to Nature, Art:
I warm'd both hands before the fire of life;
It sinks, and I am ready to depart.
                                          —Walter Savage Landor

From the Heart . . .

When prayers are so many
    and feelings so high,
When Time is so hard and Pain so near,
    You look around and feel
    that a Christian is near.
The doorbell rings and a Christian is there,
    With pots and pans and food to share,
With soft-spoken words we need to hear . . .
    "We have so much love
    and food to share . . ."
    A Christian we know is there.
    A tear or two we shouldn't fear,
    For God knows Heaven is near.

We thank God that we always
Have someone with love in their hearts
    and time to care!
                                          —Charlie M. Bradshaw

Go From Me

Go from me. Yet I feel that I shall stand
Henceforward in thy shadow. Nevermore
Alone upon the threshold of my door
Of individual life, I shall command
The uses of my soul, nor lift my hand
Serenely in the sunshine as before,
Without the sense of that which I forbore, . . .
Thy touch upon the palm. The widest land

Doom takes to part us, leaves thy heart in mine
With pulses that beat double. What I do
And what I dream include thee, as the wine
Must taste of its own grapes. And when I sue
God for myself, he hears that name of thine,
And sees within my eyes the tears of two.
                                  —Elizabeth Barrett Browning

The Harp That Once Through Tara's Halls

The harp that once through Tara's halls
    The soul music shed,
Now hangs as mute on Tara's walls
    As if that soul were fled.
So sleeps the pride of former days,
    So glory's thrill is o'er,
And hearts that once beat high for praise
    Now feel that pulse no more!

No more to chiefs and ladies bright
    The harp of Tara swells;
The chord alone that breaks at night
    Its tale of ruin tells.
Thus Freedom now so seldom wakes,
    The only throb she gives
Is when some heart indignant breaks,
    To show that still she lives.
                                  —Thomas Moore

Herrick's Cavalier

Give me that man that dares bestride
The active sea-horse, and with pride
Through that huge field of waters ride;
Who, with his looks too, can appease
The ruffling winds and raging seas
In midst of all their outrages.
This, this a virtuous man can do,
Sail against rocks, and split them too;
Ay, and a world of pikes pass through.
                                  —Robert Herrick

High Flight

Oh! I have slipped the surly bonds of Earth,
And danced the skies on laughter-silvered wings;
Sunward I've climbed, and joined the tumbling mirth
Of sun-split clouds, and done a hundred things
You have not dreamed of—wheeled and soared and swung
High in the sunlit silence. Hov'ring there,
I've chased the shouting wind along, and flung
My eager craft through footless halls of air. . . .
Up, up the long delirious, burning blue
I've topped the wind-swept heights with easy grace,
Where never lark or even eagle flew;
And while with silent, lifting mind I've trod
The high untrespassed sanctity of space,
Put out my hand and touched the face of God.

—John Magee

I Know That My Redeemer Lives

I know that my Redeemer lives,
    And ever prays for me;
A token of his love he gives,
    A pledge of liberty.

I find him lifting up my head;
    He brings salvation near;
His presence makes me free indeed,
    And he will soon appear.

He wills that I should holy be;
    What can withstand his will?
The counsel of his grace in me
    He surely shall fulfill.

When God is mine, and I am his,
    Of paradise possessed,
I taste unutterable bliss,
    And everlasting rest.

—Charles Wesley

The Journey Onwards

As slow our ship her foamy track
  Against the wind was cleaving,
Her trembling pennant still look'd back
  To that dear isle 'twas leaving.
So loth we part from all we love,
  From all the links that bind us;
So turn our hearts, as on we rove,
  To those we've left behind us!

When, round the bowl, of vanished years
  We talk with joyous seeming—
With smiles that might as well be tears,
  So faint, so sad their beaming;
While memory brings us back again
  Each early tie that twined us,
Oh, sweet's the cup that circles then
  To those we've left behind us!

And when in other climes we meet
  Some isle or vale enchanting,
Where all looks flowery, wild, and sweet,
  And nought but love is wanting;
We think how great had been our bliss
  If Heaven had but assign'd us
To live and die in scenes like this,
  With some we've left behind us!

As travelers oft look back at eve
  When eastward darkly going,
To gaze upon that light they leave
  Still faint behind them glowing,
So, when the close of pleasure's day
  To gloom hath near consign'd us,
We turn to catch one fading ray
  Of joy that's left behind us.
                                    —Thomas Moore

Life! I Know Not What Thou Art

Life! I know not what thou art,
But know that thou and I must part;

And when, or how, or where we met
I own to me's a secret yet.
 Life! We've been long together
Through pleasant and through cloudy weather;
'Tis hard to part when friends are dear—
Perhaps 'twill cost a sigh, a tear;
—Then steal away, give little warning,
 Choose thine own time;
Say not Good Night, but in some brighter clime
 Bid me Good Morning.
—Anna Letitia Barbauld

LXIII

O threats of Hell and Hopes of Paradise!
One thing at least is certain—*This* Life flies;
 One thing is certain and the rest is Lies;
The Flower that once has blown for ever dies.
—Edward Fitzgerald
From the *Rubáiyát of Omar Khayyám*

LXIV

Strange, is it not? that of the myriads who
Before us passed the door of Darkness through,
 Not one returns to tell us of the Road,
Which to discover we must travel too.
—Edward Fitzgerald
From the *Rubáiyát of Omar Khayyám*

The Man Named Legion

The man named Legion asks for nothing more
Than his own rooftree, and the right to stand
Erect, unthreatened, on a square of land,
His children sturdy and his peace secure.
The world is wide, the generous earth could nourish
All men, and more, and still have room to spare.
So brief a while is his to breathe the air,
So cheap, so simple, all that he would cherish.

Out of such modest stuff his dreams are made,
But being humble, he is set at nought;

Harried, despoiled, most grievously betrayed.
And the pathetic little that he sought
Is held beyond his hope, beyond his touch—
That little, that impossible too much!
                    —Sara Henderson Hay

Monody

To have known him, to have loved him
    After loneness long;
And then to be estranged in life,
    And neither in the wrong;
And now for death to set his seal—
    Ease me, a little ease, my song!

By wintry hills his hermit-mound
    The sheeted snow-drifts drape,
And houseless there the snow-bird flits
    Beneath the fir-trees' crape:
Glazed now with ice the cloistral vine
    That hid the shyest grape.
                    —Herman Melville

O Captain! My Captain!

O Captain! my Captain! our fearful trip is done,
The ship has weathered every rack, the prize we sought is won,
The port is near, the bells I hear, the people all exulting,
While follow eyes the steady keel, the vessel grim and daring;
    But O heart! heart! heart!
        O the bleeding drops of red,
            Where on the deck my Captain lies,
                Fallen cold and dead.

O Captain! my Captain! rise up and hear the bells;
Rise up—for you the flag is flung—for you the bugle trills,
For you bouquets and ribboned wreaths—for you the shores
        acrowding,
For you they call, the swaying mass, their eager faces turning;
    Here Captain! dear father!

This arm beneath your head!
It is some dream that on the deck
You've fallen cold and dead.

My Captain does not answer, his lips are pale and still,
My father does not feel my arm, he has no pulse nor will,
The ship is anchored safe and sound, its voyage closed and done,
From fearful trip the victor ship comes in with object won;
Exult O shores, and ring O bells!
But I with mournful tread,
Walk the deck my Captain lies,
Fallen cold and dead.

—Walt Whitman

Oh, Yet We Trust

Oh, yet we trust that somehow good
Will be the final goal of ill,
To pangs of nature, sins of will,
Defects of doubt, and taints of blood;

That nothing walks with aimless feet;
That not one life shall be destroyed,
Or cast as rubbish to the void,
When God hath made the pile complete;

That not a worm is cloven in vain;
That not a moth with vain desire
Is shrivelled in a fruitless fire,
Or but subserves another's gain.

Behold, we know not anything;
I can but trust that good shall fall
At last—far off—at last, to all,
And every winter change to spring.

So runs my dream: but what am I?
An infant crying in the night:
An infant crying for the light:
And with no language but a cry.

—Alfred, Lord Tennyson

The Old Familiar Faces

I have had playmates, I have had companions
In my days of childhood, in my joyful school-days;
All, all are gone, the old familiar faces.

I have been laughing, I have been carousing,
Drinking late, sitting late, with my bosom cronies;
All, all are gone, the old familiar faces.

I loved a love once, fairest among women:
Closed are her doors on me, I must not see her—
All, all are gone, the old familiar faces.

I have a friend, a kinder friend has no man:
Like an ingrate, I left my friend abruptly;
Left him, to muse on the old familiar faces.

Ghost-like I paced round the haunts of my childhood,
Earth seem'd a desert I was bound to traverse,
Seeking to find the old familiar faces.

Friend of my bosom, thou more than a brother,
Why wert not thou born in my father's dwelling?
So might we talk of the old familiar faces.

How some they have died, and some they have left me,
And some are taken from me; all are departed;
All, all are gone, the old familiar faces.
                                        —Charles Lamb

On an Infant Dying as Soon as Born

I saw where in the shroud did lurk
A curious frame of Nature's work;
A flow'ret crushed in the bud,
A nameless piece of Babyhood,
Was in her cradle-coffin lying;
Extinct, with scarce the sense of dying:
So soon to exchange the imprisoning womb
For darker closets of the tomb!

She did but ope an eye, and put
A clear beam forth, then straight up shut
For the long dark: ne'er more to see
Through glasses of mortality.
Riddle of destiny, who can show
What thy short visit meant, or know
What thy errand here below?
Shall we say, that Nature blind
Check'd her hand, and changed her mind,
Just when she had exactly wrought
A finish'd pattern without fault?
Could she flag, or could she tire,
Or lack'd she the Promethean fire
(With her nine moons' long workings sicken'd)
That should thy little limbs have quicken'd?
Limbs so firm, they seemed to assure
Life of health, and days mature;
Woman's self in miniature!
Limbs so fair, they might supply
(Themselves now but cold imagery)
The sculptor to make Beauty by.
Or did the stern-eyed Fate descry
That babe or mother, one must die;
So in mercy left the stock
And cut the branch; to save the shock
Of young years widow'd, and the pain
When Single State comes back again
To the lone man who, 'reft of wife,
Thenceforward drags a maiméd life?
The economy of Heaven is dark,
And wisest clerks have miss'd the mark,
Why human buds, like this, should fall
More brief than fly ephemeral
That has his day; while shrivell'd crones
Stiffen with age to stocks and stones;
And crabbéd use the conscience sears
In sinners of an hundred years.
Mother's prattle, mother's kiss,
Baby fond, thou ne'er wilt miss:

Rites, which custom does impose,
Silver bells, and baby clothes;
Coral redder than those lips
Which pale death did late eclipse;
Music framed for infants' glee,
Whistle never tuned for thee;
Though thou want'st not, thou shalt have them,
Loving hearts were they which gave them.
Let not one be missing; nurse,
See them laid upon the hearse
Of infant slain by doom perverse.
Why should kings and nobles have
Pictured trophies to their grave,
And we, churls, to thee deny
Thy pretty toys with thee to lie—
A more harmless vanity?

—Charles Lamb

Prospice

Fear death?—to feel the fog in my throat,
    The mist in my face,
When the snows begin, and the blasts denote
    I am nearing the place,
The power of the night, the press of the storm,
    The post of the foe;
Where he stands, the Arch Fear in a visible form,
    Yet the strong man must go;
For the journey is done and the summit attained,
    And the barriers fall,
Though a battle's to fight ere the guerdon be gained,
    The reward of it all.
I was ever a fighter, so—one fight more,
    The best and the last!
I would hate that death bandaged my eyes, and forebore,
    And bade me creep past.
No! let me taste the whole of it, fare like my peers
    The heroes of old,
Bear the brunt, in a minute pay glad life's arrears
    Of pain, darkness and cold.
For sudden the worst turns the best to the brave,

The black minute's at end,
And the elements' rage, the fiend-voices that rave,
    Shall dwindle, shall blend,
Shall change, shall become first a peace out of pain,
    Then a light, then thy breast,
O thou soul of my soul! I shall clasp thee again,
    And with God be the rest!

—Robert Browning

Rabbi Ben Ezra

Grow old along with me!
The best is yet to be,
The last of life, for which the first was made:
Our times are in his hand
Who saith, "A whole I planned,
Youth shows but half; trust God: see all, nor be afraid!"

—Robert Browning

Revolutions

Like as the waves make towards the pebbled shore,
So do our minutes hasten to their end;
Each changing place with that which goes before,
In sequent toil all forwards do contend.
Nativity, once in the main of light,
Crawls to maturity, wherewith being crown'd,
Crooked eclipses 'gainst his glory fight,
And Time that gave doth now his gift confound.
Time doth transfix the flourish set on youth,
And delves the parallels in beauty's brow;
Feeds on the rarities of nature's truth,
And nothing stands but for his scythe to mow:
And yet, to times in hope, my verse shall stand
Praising thy worth, despite his cruel hand.

—William Shakespeare

Requiescat

Strew on her roses, roses,
    And never a spray of yew.
In quiet she reposes:
    Ah! would that I did too.

Her mirth the world required:
　　She bathed it in smiles of glee.
But her heart was tired, tired,
　　And now they let her be.

Her life was turning, turning,
　　In mazes of heat and sound.
But for peace her soul was yearning,
　　And now peace laps her round.

Her cabined, ample spirit,
　　It fluttered and failed for breath.
Tonight it doth inherit
　　The vasty hall of death.
　　　　　　　　　　—Matthew Arnold

The River of Life

The more we live, more brief appear
　　Our life's succeeding stages:
A day to childhood seems a year,
　　And years like passing ages.

The gladsome current of our youth,
　　Ere passion yet disorders,
Steals lingering like a river smooth
　　Along its grassy borders.

But as the careworn cheek grows wan,
　　And sorrow's shafts fly thicker,
Ye stars, that measure life to man,
　　Why seem your courses quicker?

When joys have lost their bloom and breath,
　　And life itself is vapid,
Why, as we reach the falls of death,
　　Feel we its tide more rapid?

It may be strange—yet who would change
　　Time's course to slower speeding,
When one by one our friends have gone
　　And left our bosoms bleeding?

Heaven gives our years of fading strength
   Indemnifying fleetness;
And those of youth, a seeming length,
   Proportioned to their sweetness.
                   —Thomas Campbell

Soldier, Rest

Soldier, rest! thy warfare o'er,
   Sleep the sleep that knows not breaking;
Dream of battled fields no more,
   Days of danger, nights of waking.
In our isle's enchanted hall,
   Hands unseen thy couch are strewing,
Fairy strains of music fall,
   Every sense in slumber dewing.
Soldier, rest! thy warfare o'er,
Dream of fighting fields no more;
Sleep the sleep that knows not breaking,
Morn of toil, nor night of waking.

No rude sound shall reach thine ear,
   Armor's clang, or war-steed champing,
Trump nor pibroch summon here
   Mustering clan, or squadron tramping.
Yet the lark's shrill fife may come
   At the daybreak from the fallow,
And the bittern sound his drum,
   Booming from the sedgy shallow.
Ruder sounds shall none be near,
Guards nor warders challenge here;
Here's no war-steed's neigh and champing,
Shouting clans or squadrons stamping.

Huntsman, rest! thy chase is done,
   While our slumbrous spells assail ye,
Dream not, with the rising sun,
   Bugles here shall sound reveille.
Sleep! the deer is in his den;
   Sleep! thy hounds are by thee lying;
Sleep! nor dream in yonder glen
   How thy gallant steed lay dying.

Huntsman, rest! thy chase is done;
Think not of the rising sun,
For, at dawning to assail ye,
Here no bugles sound reveille.

Sir Walter Scott
—from *The Lady of the Lake*

Tempt Me No More

Tempt me no more; for I
Have known the lightning's hour,
The poet's inward pride,
The certainty of power.

Bayonets are closing round.
I shrink; yet I must wring
A living from despair
And out of steel a song.

Though song, though breath be short,
I'll share not the disgrace
Of those that ran away
Or never left the base.

Comrades, my tongue can speak
No comfortable words;
Calls to a forlorn hope
Give work and not rewards.

O keep the sickle sharp
And follow still the plow:
Others may reap, though some
See not the winter through.

Father who endest all,
Pity our broken sleep;
For we lie down with tears
And waken but to weep.

And if our blood alone
Will meet this iron earth,
Take it. It is well spent
Easing a savior's birth.

—C. Day Lewis

Thanatopsis

To him who in the love of Nature holds
Communion with her visible forms, she speaks
A various language; for his gayer hours
She has a voice of gladness, and a smile
And eloquence of beauty; and she glides
Into his darker musings, with a mild
And healing sympathy that steals away
Their sharpness ere he is aware. When thoughts
Of the last bitter hour come like a blight
Over thy spirit, and sad images
Of the stern agony, and shroud and pall
And breathless darkness and the narrow house
Make thee to shudder and grow sick at heart,
Go forth under the open sky and list
To Nature's teachings, while from all around—
Earth and her waters and the depths of air—
Comes a still voice:
Yet a few days, and thee
The all-beholding sun shall see no more
In all his course; nor yet in the cold ground,
Where thy pale form was laid with many tears,
Nor in the embrace of ocean, shall exist
Thy image. Earth, that nourished thee shall claim
Thy growth, to be resolved to earth again,
And, lost each human trace, surrendering up
Thine individual being, shalt thou go
To mix for ever with the elements,
To be a brother to the insensible rock
And to the sluggish clod, which the rude swain
Turns with his share, and treads upon; the oak
Shall send his roots abroad, and pierce thy mould.

Yet not to thine eternal resting-place
Shalt thou retire alone, nor couldst thou wish
Couch more magnificent. Thou shalt lie down
With patriarchs of the infant world, with kings,
The powerful of the earth, the wise, the good,
Fair forms, and hoary seers of ages past,
All in one mighty sepulchre. The hills
Rock-ribbed and ancient as the sun; the vales
Stretching in pensive quietness between;
The venerable woods, rivers that move
In majesty, and the complaining brooks
That make the meadows green; and, poured round all,
Old Ocean's gray and melancholy waste,—
Are but the solemn decorations all
Of the great tomb of man. The golden sun,
The planets, all the infinite host of heaven,
Are shining on the sad abodes of death,
Through the still lapse of ages. All that tread
The globe are but a handful to the tribes
That slumber in its bosom. Take the wings
Of morning, pierce the Barcan wilderness,
Or lose thyself in the contiguous woods
Where rolls the Oregon, and hears no sound
Save his own dashings; yet the dead are there,
And millions in those solitudes, since first
The flight of years began, have laid them down
In their last sleep: the dead reign there alone.
So shalt thou rest; and what if thou withdraw
In silence from the living, and no friend
Take note of thy departure? All that breathe
Will share thy destiny. The gay will laugh
When thou art gone, the solemn brood of care
Plod on, and each one as before will chase
His favorite phantom; yet all these shall leave
Their mirth and their employments, and shall come
And make their bed with thee. As the long train
Of ages glide away, the sons of men—
The youth in life's green spring, and he who goes
In the full strength of years, matron and maid,
The speechless babe, and the gray-headed man—

Shall one by one be gathered to thy side
By those who in their turn shall follow them.
So live that when thy summons come to join
The innumerable caravan which moves
To that mysterious realm where each shall take
His chamber in the silent halls of death,
Thou go not, like the quarry-slave at night,
Scourged to his dungeon, but, sustained and soothed
By an unfaltering trust, approach thy grave
Like one who wraps the drapery of his couch
About him and lies down to pleasant dreams.

—William Cullen Bryant

When I Have Fears That I May Cease to Be

When I have fears that I may cease to be
   Before my pen has gleaned my teeming brain,
Before high pilèd books, in charact'ry
   Hold like rich garners the full ripened grain;
When I behold, upon the night's starred face,
   Huge cloudy symbols of a high romance,
And think that I may never live to trace
   Their shadows, with the magic hand of chance;
And when I feel, fair creature of an hour,
   That I shall never look upon thee more,
Never have relish in the faery power
   Of unreflecting love;—then on the shore
Of the wide world I stand alone, and think
   Till love and fame to nothingness do sink.

—John Keats

Youth and Age

Verse, a breeze 'mid blossoms straying,
   Where Hope clung feeding, like a bee—
Both were mine! Life went a-maying
   . With Nature, Hope, and Poesy,
      When I was young.

When I was young? Ah, woeful When.
Ah, for the change 'twixt Now and Then!

This breathing house not built with hands,
        This body that does me grievous wrong,
O'er aery cliffs and glittering sands
        How lightly then it flash'd along:
Like those trim skiffs, unknown of yore,
        On winding lakes and rivers wide,
That ask no aid of sail or oar,
        That fear no spite of wind or tide!
Nought cared this body for wind or weather
When Youth and I lived in't together.

Flowers are lovely; Love is flower-like;
        Friendship is a sheltering tree;
O! the joys, that came down shower-like,
        Of Friendship, Love, and Liberty,
                Ere I was old!

Ere I was old? Ah, woeful Ere,
Which tells me, Youth's no longer here!
O Youth! for years so many and sweet
        'Tis known that Thou and I were one,
I'll think it but a fond conceit—
        It cannot be that thou art gone!
Thy vesper bell hath not yet toll'd:
And thou wert ay a masker bold!
What strange disguise hast now put on
To make believe that thou art gone?
I see these locks in silvery slips,
        This drooping gait, this alter'd size:
But Springtide blossoms on thy lips,
        And tears take sunshine from thine eyes!
Life is but thought: so think I will
That Youth and I are housemates still.

Dew-drops are the gems of morning,
        But the tears of mournful eve!
Where no hope is, life's a warning
        That only serves to make us grieve
                When we are old:

That only serves to make us grieve
With oft and tedious taking-leave,
Like some poor nigh-related guest
That may not rudely be dismist,
Yet hath outstay'd of his welcome while,
And tells the jest without the smile.
                              —Samuel Taylor Coleridge

The following selections are from *Found,* by Pearl Pierson

Though darkness ever grows more dense
We know that Light will come, and hence
This gathering darkness but portends
That coming Day when darkness ends!
We look upon the earth, and sigh—
We lift our eyes: Hope tints the sky
With dawning Light; and each bright ray
Brings richer promise of the Day—
    God Is—God Is—GOD IS!

A widow, grieving for her son,
An act of tender mercy done,
'Twas thus the Master's race was run.
Man's trust in God was thus begun:
And thus man's faith today is won.

A kindly word of sympathy,
A whisper of eternity—
'Tis thus our soul is made to see
That Christ has power to set us free—
'Tis thus, dear Lord, we come to Thee.

He does not fear the raging sea,
As on the breast of Galilee,
Serene and calm, and Spirit free,
    Our Saviour sleeps.

Ah, why should any mortal fear
The winds of life? the Lord is near;
He speaks in accents calm and clear:
    Believe in me.

We find new hope when we confess
Dependence on His righteousness:
In times of storm, or deep distress,
    He giveth peace.

In cycle growth, life moves along:
    The seed, the leaf, the plant, the bloom—
Then seed again, which does not grow
Until it rises from its tomb
In which it leaves its outer shell.
    The kernel, where life must begin,
Grows warm with hope of coming spring—
    And life revives, where life has been.

We live, (or think we live,) until
    We realize that we must die:
We must forsake these earthly shells,
    E'er Living Water can supply
Eternal life to souls within
    These outer shells of earthy clay—
Yes, we must die to things of earth
    To find our resurrection day.

Forever the accepted time
Is now! The onward, upward climb
Grows brighter every step we take—
As happier, more wide awake
We hasten to behold the face
Of Him who saves us by His grace.
With grace He doth our hearts endow
To live in the eternal now.

Eternity is very real,
When through the Spirit we can feel
The wounded hand of him who gave
His life to lift us from the grave:
And oh, how glorious grows the way
When we have learned to live today!
Yes, Jesus came to teach us how
To live in the eternal now.

O loving Father, give us seeing eyes!
We view the glory of Thy arching skies,
And know that in Thy house no darkness is—
For Christ is Light; and all Thy mansions His.
We do not live until we see His light
And glory in the greatness of His might!

When we suffer grief and anguish,
    To our hearts, now wracked with pain,
Comes the oft repeated question,
    Did the Master die in vain?

No! He died to save the spirits
    Living in the haunts of death—
Jesus is the resurrection!
    There is healing in His breath!

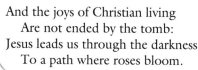

Life is found amidst destruction—
    Gold is found amidst alloy—
Thus our path of pain and sorrow
    Leads, through Christ, to heights of joy.

And the joys of Christian living
    Are not ended by the tomb:
Jesus leads us through the darkness
    To a path where roses bloom.

Some day the Master Shepherd
    Will come to claim His own;
And there will be rejoicing
    Where ever He is known:
How blest will be that shepherd
    Whose sheep have found the way
Into that larger Sheepfold
    From which they will not stray!

O precious Shepherd of our souls,
Thy love each wandering lamb consoles.
All we like sheep have gone astray,
    And God hath laid our sins on Thee—

Yet Thou hast glorified His name
  And set our ransomed spirits free.
Thy love hath silenced fear and doubt—
Thou hast encompassed us about
With arms of love. In Thee is found
  The peace of Thy forgiving grace.
And through Thy glorious victory
  We now behold Thee, face to face!

13

Hymns

Listed in this section are the titles of 110 hymns, many of which have been used at funeral and memorial services I've conducted. Others have lyrics I believe are suitable. These can be found in contemporary hymnals. Of course, the list is not exhaustive.

Families are often so dazed and numb that it is hard for them to recollect and think. Remembering the titles of hymns the deceased would have liked or chosen may be difficult. You can be of assistance by providing the titles of several hymns from which they can choose. Make sure, however, that the musicians performing at the service know the songs and/or have the music available.

I always suggest that the sadder songs be used in the first part of the service and the more hopeful, upbeat songs be used at the close to affirm the resurrection.

Occasionally, families will request classical music, such as Beethoven and Mozart. You may also have families request popular songs. You will have to decide the appropriateness based on content of the words.

Abide with Me
Abide with Me; 'tis Eventide
Above the Bright Blue
Amazing Grace
An Empty Mansion
As the Life of a Flower
Asleep in Jesus
At Evening Time

Be Not Dismayed
Be with Me, Lord
Beautiful Isle of Somewhere
Beautiful Valley of Eden
Because He Lives
Beyond the Sunset
Beyond this Land of Parting
Blessed Assurance
Brief Life Is Here Our Portion

Come, Ye Disconsolate

Does Jesus Care?

Every Cloud Has a Silver Lining
Eternal Father, Strong to Save

Face to Face
Farther Along
For All the Saints

Going Home
God Shall Wipe Away
God Will Take Care of You
God's Tomorrow

Haven of Rest
Heaven
Heaven Holds All to Me
Heaven Will Surely Be
Home of the Soul
How Beautiful Heaven Must Be
How Great Thou Art

I Have Heard of a Land
I Know My Heavenly Father Knows
I Know Not Why God's Wondrous Grace
I'll Fly Away
I'll Meet You in the Morning
I'm a Pilgrim
If We Never Meet Again
Immortal Love, Forever Full
In Heavenly Love Abiding
In the Garden
In the Land of Fadeless Day
In the Shadow of His Wings
It Is Well With My Soul

Jesus, Rose of Sharon
Jesus Knows and Cares
Just a Rose Will Do

Lead, Kindly Light

My God and I
My Soul in Sad Exile

Near to the Heart of God
Nearer, My God, to Thee

Nearer, Still Nearer
Never Grow Old
No Tears in Heaven
Nobody Knows But Jesus
Not Now But in the Coming Years

O Heart, Bowed Down with Sorrow
O Love that Wilt Not Let Me Go
Oh, They Tell Me of a Home
Oh, Think of the Home Over There
One Sweetly Solemn Thought
Only in Thee

Peace, Perfect Peace
Precious Lord, Take My Hand
Precious Memories
Prepare to Meet Thy God

Rock of Ages

Safe in the Arms of Jesus
Safe in the Harbor
Saved by Grace
Shall We Gather at the River?
Shall We Meet Beyond?
Someday the Silver Cord Will Break
Sometime We'll Understand
Sunset and Evening Star
Sweet Peace, the Gift of God's Love

Tarry with Me
That Heavenly Home
The Last Mile of the Way

The Old Rugged Cross
The Sands Have Been Washed
The Sands of Time
The Touch of His Hand on Mine
The Way of the Cross
There Are Loved Ones
There Will Be Light
There's a Land Beyond the River
There's a Land that Is Fairer (Sweet By and By)
This World Is Not My Home
Thou My Everlasting Portion
To Canaan's Land I'm on My Way

Under His Wings
Unto the Hills

Victory in Jesus

We Are Going Down
We Shall Meet Someday
What a Friend We Have in Jesus
When All My Labors and Trials
When Comes to the Weary a Blessed Release
When Day's Shadows
When I Shall Come
When the Roll Is Called Up Yonder
Where the Roses Never Fade
Will the Circle Be Unbroken?

Yes, for Me

14

Committal Services

Example of a Committal Prayer

Dear Heavenly Father:

It is difficult for us to say goodbye to _____. We now commit him/her to your care, knowing and acknowledging that you are the God of all the universe, that you have created us and redeemed us in Christ, and that you are always a God of love and compassion.

We pray that you will console and comfort this family (use names where appropriate). Help them in their pain, tears, and loss to see you and your love and to understand you more completely. Please surround them with your warm, loving arms of compassion.

We know that you will call us all before you on that great, final day. Help us to find our confidence in our Lord and Savior, Jesus Christ, who died for us, who won complete victory over death for us, and who taught us to say: (recite here the Lord's Prayer if you so desire, and close in Jesus' name).

Committal Service Poetry

The following poems were written by my aunt Pearl Pierson when her son was accidentally killed. I believe any of them would be appropriate to read at a committal service.

Reason for Our Hope

Those loving eyes are closed in sleep;
Yet we have hope, and do not weep
For him who goes to dwell above
Where all is joy, and peace and love.

That tongue, whose gentle kindly word
The eager little children heard,
Is quiet now; yet we rejoice
In hope again to hear that voice.

Those active hands no longer toil
Amid the rocky earthly soil:
We view the fruitage of their work,
And thank the Lord they did not shirk.

Those ready feet, so quick to run
On errands here for everyone
Are now at rest, no more to roam.
A living soul has journeyed home.

We look above with hope secure
In him whose Word is true and sure,
Eternal, endless in its scope.
We look to Christ in blessed hope.

                                        1 Peter 3:15–22

God's Eternal Love

We sorrow not as they who have no hope,
For God has given us a vision of the scope
    Of his eternal love.
What blessed hope is ours, who pray and wait
To gain an entrance to yon pearly gate!
For all our losses God will compensate.
    He lives! He reigns above!

When God so loved the world he gave
His Son to lift us from the grave.
   Should we repine and weep?
We look to God in praise, and say,
"Thy will be done." We hope and pray
For added strength from day to day
   God's holy Word to keep.

John 3:16

We Find It So

So much we do not understand—
   So much we do not know—
We trust all things with Thee, dear Lord,
   And it is better so.
Thy way will make our faith secure;
Thy way will make our hope endure;
Thy way will make our blessings sure.
   Thy way is best; we find it so.

O Father God, Thy way is best,
   And we have found it so.
We find in Thee our peace and rest;
   In Thee we live and grow.
Thy way will make us good and wise,
For in Thy way of life we rise
To dwell with Thee beyond the skies.
   Thy way is best; we find it so.

Psalm 1:1–3

His Way Is Best

His way is best, we find it so.
There is so much we do not know.
We trust in God and find sweet rest:
Whatever comes, his way is best.

His way is best. We do not grieve
When sorrow comes, for we believe
That righteous souls awaken blest.
We have bright hope. God's way is best.

His way is best. He conquered death.
He gives our souls eternal breath.
He gives us strength to meet each test.
We trust in God. His way is best.

His way is best. It always is.
He cares for us for we are his.
He comforts all who have confessed
Their trust in him. His way is best.

Proverbs 3:5–6; 4:18

A Great Experience

A great experience awaits
The living soul at heaven's gates,
Yet still with trembling heart we fear
The hand of death as it draws near.

The great experience of death
But robs our frame of mortal breath,
And gives our soul a full release
To rise to joyous lands of peace.

The great experience of life,
Beyond all sorrow, pain, and strife,
Is worth our toil and struggle here,
And all that mortal man holds dear.

A great experience above
Awaits for all who know the love
Of him who rules the earth and sky,
And calls us home to dwell on high.

Philippians 1:21

Remember, O Father, that I am of clay;
Thou gavest me life, thou canst take it away.
In Jesus I glory, for I am so weak.
Oh, give me the wisdom I earnestly seek.
All honor and power and glory are thine;
Oh, grant me a portion of riches divine.
Thy grace fills my soul with thine infinite love,

Yet still I am seeking more light from above.
I praise thee for blessings again and again.
May thine be the glory forever. Amen.

In Thy Hand

I did not know which way to go
  to reach the Promised Land.
I heard One say, "I am the way";
  then Jesus took my hand.

My light was dim, I turned to him;
  he helped me understand.
The Master came and spoke my name;
  he took my trembling hand.

O God above, how sweet thy love!
  I seek thy blest command.
Thy will for me, oh let it be
  forever in thy hand.

Until the end, O Savior Friend,
  all things are in thy hand.
Thy love divine has made me thine,
  I trust thy guiding hand.

John 14:1–21

O Death, Where Is Thy Victory

O death, where is thy victory?
  O death, where is thy sting?
Thanks be to God for victory!
  In Jesus Christ we sing
Of life, sweet life, abundant life,
  Of life beyond the grave.
We have eternal life in Christ,
  The life he freely gave.

O grave, where is thy victory?
  O death, where is thy power?
Thanks be to God for victory,
  For strength to meet each hour!

In Christ we find the way of life—
The joyous glory-way
To shining mansions in the skies
Where we may dwell someday.

For death there is no victory!
The sting of earthly sin
Is swallowed up in victory!
Through Christ we enter in
The glories of eternal life.
Though still on earth we trod,
We know that we have found the way
To endless life with God.

1 Corinthians 15:50–57